Alaska
CURIOSITIES

Help Us Keep This Guide Up to Date

Every effort has been made by the author and editors to make this guide as accurate and useful as possible. However, many things can change after a guide is published—establishments close, phone numbers change, hiking trails are rerouted, facilities come under new management, etc.

We would love to hear from you concerning your experiences with this guide and how you feel it could be improved and kept up to date. While we may not be able to respond to all comments and suggestions, we'll take them to heart, and we'll also make certain to share them with the author. Please send your comments and suggestions to the following address:

GPP
Reader Response/Editorial Department
PO Box 480
Guilford, CT 06437

Or you may e-mail us at:
editorial@GlobePequot.com
Thanks for your input, and happy travels!

Curiosities Series

Alaska
CURIOSITIES

Quirky characters,
roadside oddities &
other offbeat stuff

B. B. Mackenzie

Guilford, Connecticut

The prices and rates in this guidebook were confirmed at press time. We recommend, however, that you call establishments before traveling to obtain current information.

To buy books in quantity for corporate use or incentives, call **(800) 962–0973** or e-mail **premiums@GlobePequot.com**.

All photos by the author unless otherwise noted.
Maps by Daniel Lloyd © Morris Book Publishing, LLC
Text design: Bret Kerr
Project editor: Meredith Dias
Layout: Casey Shain

ISSN 2165-9184

ISBN 978-0-7627-7009-0

Printed in the United States of America

10 9 8 7 6 5 4 3 2 1

To Mike, who keeps me curious

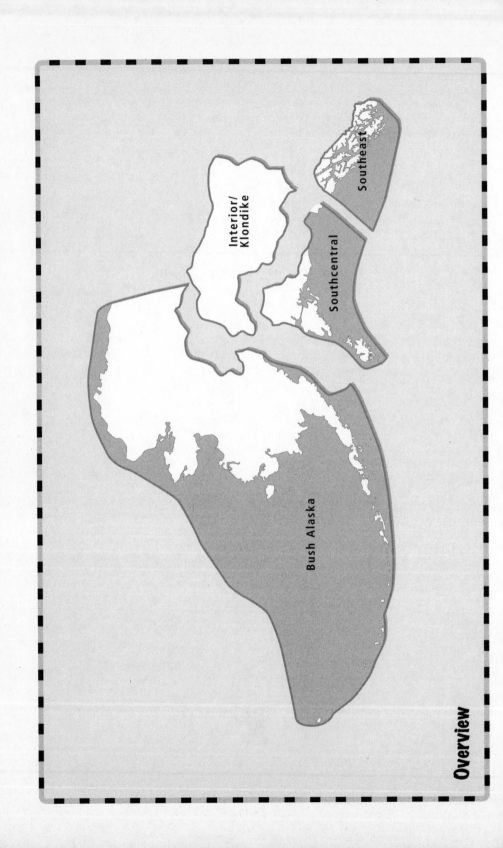

Interior/
Klondike

Southeast

Southcentral

Bush Alaska

Overview

contents

acknowledgments

★ ★

Alaska is a grand and welcoming place, filled with generous people to whom I'm grateful on a daily basis. For this project, my thanks especially to photographers Kaela Tanner, Gail Giles, Seth Kantner, and G. M. Ferency.

introduction

★ ★

*R*ounding up Alaska's curiosities feels a little like cheating, because there's so much of the curious here. Larger than life, chilly, remote, Alaska is full of the capacity to amaze. "There are strange things done in the midnight sun," said poet Robert Service, and you'd be hard-pressed to find an Alaskan who disagrees.

One of the toughest parts of researching this book is that we Alaskans take for granted things others find pretty strange. In the Bush, you can't drive from one town to the next. A frozen waterway might be as close as you get to a highway, and so taxicabs run up and down some rivers in January. Where we can drive, it's with electrical cords flapping from under our hoods, because without plugging them in, our cars don't like to start in the cold.

At twenty below, propane thickens. At forty below, fuel oil gels, and the curiosity curve steepens. Tires thump-thump on the road when rubber flattens and freezes. Droplets of water from our exhaled breath and engine exhaust thicken to ice fog so dense you're unable to see even your freezing toes. Hot liquid tossed in the air disappears before hitting the ground.

But it's not only the cold that gets people scratching their heads. In Anchorage, you're as likely to see a moose on the loose as you are a stray dog. "Hey Bear" is a common call in our parks. For fun we run with reindeer, compete for bachelors in auctions, play softball on snowshoes, and don fur bikinis to break the midwinter blahs.

Spread over our 586,000 square miles are more than a few quirky individuals with unusual pastimes and passions. In Nome they race bathtubs. Near Homer they sell coffee from a floating espresso shop. In Palmer they make vodka from salmon. In Anchorage they dress up in duct tape and dance. People who to us don't seem so extraordinary—fishermen, gold miners, bush pilots, state troopers, even one half-term governor—attract curious audiences on reality TV.

Our history's full of curiosities, too. You don't often hear of men who'd make thirty or forty trips up a mountain hauling fifty pounds of supplies on their backs, but thousands did exactly that in the 1898 rush for gold. We've got our ghost towns and even a ghost train, left to rust on the windswept tundra. We've even got Wyatt Earp's pistol, checked but never claimed.

If that weren't abundance enough, we've got curious natural phenomena. Mountain-flattening Fata Morgana. Mysterious aurora that bounce reds, greens, and pinks in the sky. Binky the shoe-eating polar bear. Tiny beetles that freeze to far below zero and live to go another round the next spring. And most curious of all things, an elephant with her own treadmill and bumper stickers.

Alaska's a curious place, and we Alaskans like it that way. It's been all too much fun exploring what just comes naturally to us.

Southeast Alaska

Access, or lack of it, makes Alaska unique, and that goes for Southeast Alaska as much as it does for the Bush. Though it's close to the rest of the continental United States (the Lower 48, in Alaska speak), Southeast Alaska is none too easy to get to. Hemmed in by mountains on the east and a coastline jagged with fjords to the west, most of Southeast can be reached only by air or by water. The state runs a Marine Highway System to transport passengers and vehicles from town to town, so folks don't go broke flying themselves in and out of places like Ketchikan, Sitka, and Petersburg. Our politicians have had endless fun threatening to move the state capital from Juneau so constituents could actually drive to it.

This skinny, mountainous, coastal part of Alaska is also called the Panhandle, which makes sense if you think of the main part of the state as a pot flipped over the Bering Sea and the Pacific. The scenery is reminiscent of Scandinavia, with rocky beaches, thick spruce and hemlock forests, towering waterfalls, and abundant marine wildlife. If it weren't for the limestone caves like the sprawling El Capitan on Prince of Wales Island, you'd never know that long ago chunks of what's now Southeast Alaska were shoved north by shifting tectonic plates, lining up our geological history with that of the South Pacific.

Southeast has its mysteries, including which long-ago people left their mark at Wrangell's Petroglyph Park, and who can claim the Ice

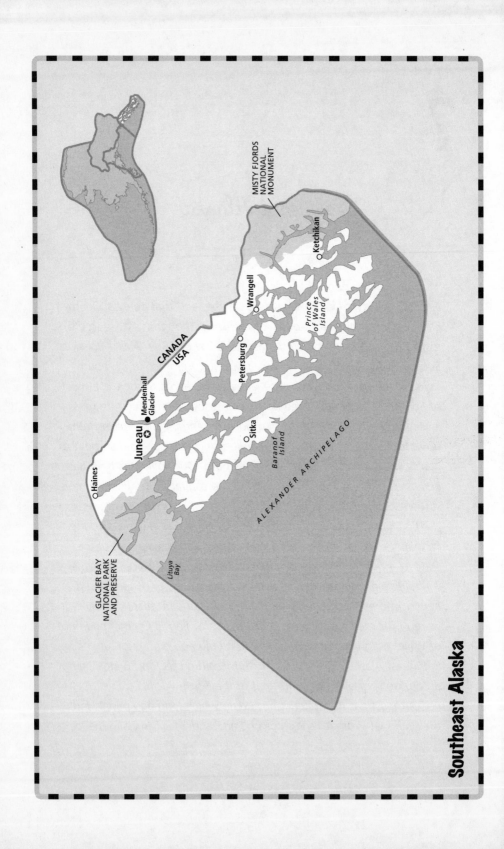

Southeast Alaska

Man Mummy among their ancestors. In the frenzy of fishing and logging that brought a later influx to Southeast, married men snuck off on their own designated trail to visit the good-time girls of Ketchikan's Creek District. Dealing with a more serious transgression, a married couple acted as judge, jury, and executioner of a murderer at Lituya Bay one isolated winter. The gold rush brought the desperate, the hopeful, the con men. If the tales are true, it left some Southeast hotels and saloons with a ghost or two.

Present-day Southeast Alaska has its quirky artists and local personalities, including a black wolf that befriended Juneau dogs and their owners before he met a bad end. For a string of quiet communities, the region has also gotten some unwitting attention through political wrangling over Ketchikan's infamous Bridge to Nowhere and Juneau's oft-tapped Baranof Suite 604.

Today there are really two Southeast Alaskas—one when cruise ships pull into port, spilling tourists eager for diamonds and T-shirts and sights, and one apart from the crowds, where longtime Alaskans quietly live and work and share a sense of community in a place that's beyond extraordinary. Curiosities inhabit both versions. Come in on the tide and explore. You won't leave disappointed.

Alaska's Mystery Seafood

Among Alaska's greatest treasures: our seafood. Wild, tasty salmon—five different kinds, prized not only for flavor but also for their healthy omega-3 fatty acids. Flat, diamond-shaped halibut with eyes that migrate to one side so they can feed along the floor of the ocean. Plump shrimp and sprawling king crab. In Southeast Alaska, there's an abundance of seafood of all types.

When it comes to the ocean's harvest, taste trumps appearance, and that's a good thing when it comes to the sea cucumber. Sea cucumbers look like oversized slugs, slimy and spiny. But in the Asian market, sea cucumbers are a big hit.

The Alaskan sea cucumber, harvested off the ocean floor by divers near Ketchikan, resembles its vegetable namesake only in size and shape. It's like scallops or shrimp, but more mysterious. Little is known about why the sea cucumber lives where it does, or what makes it flourish, or how long it survives.

Harvesting the Alaska sea cucumber is a worthy pursuit. There are twenty areas where sea cucumbers can be taken, and the daily bag limit is a whopping two thousand pounds. Once taken up from the ocean, the meat is salted and boiled, then frozen in chunks to be shipped off to Asia.

* *

Ghost Ship *Clara Nevada*
Eldred Rock

North of the Eldred Rock lighthouse lies the wreck of the *Clara Nevada*, a ship that sank during a storm in the shallows of Lynn Canal on February 5, 1898. Ten years later, nearly to the day, a lighthouse keeper reportedly looked out after an equally ferocious storm to find the wreck and the carnage had surfaced. A short time later it disappeared.

The ghostly sighting of the ill-fated vessel is but one of many mysteries and legends surrounding the wreck. During the rush to the Klondike, ships sank all too often. In the eager rush to haul miners north to the gold fields, crews and boats were hastily assembled, with many men and vessels having no business at sea. On the *Clara Nevada*'s

An archival photo of the *Clara Nevada*, originally known as the *Hassler*, a boat considered too old to be seaworthy
ALASKA STATE LIBRARY, WINTER AND POND
PHOTOGRAPH COLLECTION, ASL-P87-1594

★ ★

maiden voyage, there were multiple complaints about her drunken crew and her unsafe conditions, including lanterns that tipped and boilers that were unfit for service.

Despite the rocky trip north, the *Clara Nevada* unloaded at Skagway and picked up an unknown number of passengers. Still hauling dynamite the crew had failed to offload on the ship's first pass by its destination in Juneau, the *Clara Nevada* turned south again, headed into a storm it had battled on its way up Alaska's Inside Passage. The last that was seen of the vessel was a fireball reported by witnesses near Eldred Rock. Later scraps of its hull washed ashore, along with several of its life preservers, some filled with grass instead of cork. Only one body was recovered. The rest of the crew and passengers were assumed to have gone down with the ship.

Though divers have searched the wreckage, none have recovered the gold that was reported by several newspapers to have been aboard. Accounts varied, but some placed the value at $13 million in today's dollars. However, there was no certain record of any gold having been taken aboard the *Clara Nevada,* and news accounts from the Klondike are notoriously unreliable.

In his book *The "Clara Nevada,"* author Steven C. Levi speculates that murder and robbery may have been involved in the ship's demise, and that her captain somehow escaped the sinking. All that seems to be certain is that the vessel went down with plenty of secrets—and gave up none when she surfaced again.

Alaska's Doctor Doolittle
Haines

Steve Kroschel is a hard guy to miss. He's the one jabbering in a cartoon voice while a wolverine nibbles his neck. When he's not cavorting with wolverines and other Alaskan critters at the Kroschel Wildlife Center, you might find him out in the mountains, triggering avalanches.

✳ ✳

**Kroschel Wildlife Center director Steve Kroschel hams
it up with a wolverine.**
PHOTO BY RON HORN

Kroschel claims wolverines changed his life. A high cartoon-like
voice is one way he gets on their level. Experience has taught him that
the animals he keeps at his wildlife center respond better to sounds
and voices that are outside the typical range for humans. The neck bit-
ing? That's a wolverine sign of affection—sort of. It can also be how
they take down their prey. Among the largest of the weasel family,

wolverines have earned a reputation as ferocious for a mammal the size of a beaver. Still, Kroschel considers the ones at his park to be part of his family, and he'll make that apparent with an occasional wolverine smooch.

With its weathered wood buildings, the Kroschel Wildlife Center may not look like much, but it's up on all its state permits and animal inspections. What makes it special are the intimate relationships between the animals and their caretaker, an intimacy that Kroschel shares with the center's guests.

To join Kroschel for an up-close and personal tour of over fifteen species of Alaska animals, including wolf, moose, lynx, fox, grizzly bear, and of course wolverine, head twenty-eight miles north of Haines to Mile 1.8 Mosquito Lake Road. We don't recommend that you join him for his other adventurous activities, which include detonating avalanches for film crews. By comparison, wolverines seem almost tame.

Hammering Home
Haines

Despite its small population, Alaska has a healthy number of museums. In Anchorage, the Museum at Rasmuson Center showcases Alaska history and art and houses an imaginarium for children. In Fairbanks, there's the world-class Museum of the North. And in small towns from Ketchikan to Kenai to Skagway to Bethel, there are fine local museums housing artifacts and historical exhibits, showing off what's unique about the forty-ninth state.

One of these museums, however, has very little to do with Alaska. That would be the Hammer Museum in Haines, the northernmost point of the state's Marine Highway System.

Haines came into this distinction through the efforts of Dave Pahl, a longtime collector of hammers. Pahl and his wife arrived in Haines years ago, having acquired a homesite through the state's lottery

★ ★

Hammers of types you likely never imagined line the walls of the Hammer Museum in Haines.
PHOTO COURTESY OF THE HAMMER MUSEUM

system. They settled on Mosquito Lake, thirty miles outside of Haines, and set about building their homestead, which naturally involved a hammer or two. Working without electricity, Pahl became well acquainted with hand tools, and as a hobby, he began restoring them. While traveling Outside (that is, in the Lower 48 states), Pahl began poking around antiques stores and picking up old hammers. Before long he had more hammers than his house could hold.

In 2001, Pahl purchased an old building at 138 Main Street in Haines with the idea of opening a hammer museum. In keeping with his theme, he used hand tools and a wheelbarrow to restore the foundation. His efforts were rewarded with a rare find: a Tlingit stone hammer.

Even older is the collection's dolerite ball hammer from Egypt—it dates to 2500 BC, and it was likely used in the construction of one of the Giza pyramids. In addition to tools, the Hammer Museum also features machinery and documents related to a specialized industry: the manufacture of hickory hammer handles. You'll also find salesmen's samples, spring-loaded meat tenderizers, a helicopter rotor blade tapper, a hammer used to test cheese quality, and popular, practical tips on how to avoid hitting your fingers when you put your own hammer to work.

Also on display is a makeshift hammer of personal interest to Pahl. One day while launching his boat in nearby Hoonah, Pahl's truck skipped the curb and started to sink with his Australian shepherd inside. A local man swam to the rescue but wasn't able to reach the dog until someone tossed him a piece of driftwood shaped like—you guessed it—a hammer. Window broken, pooch rescued, and another exhibit makes its way into the museum.

You won't have any trouble finding the Hammer Museum. It's the only building on Main Street with a nineteen-foot hammer poised in the front yard. Pahl constructed the big hammer himself, using a spruce log twenty-six inches in diameter for the handle and carving the head from a big hunk of Styrofoam.

Despite its unusual focus, the Hammer Museum has a serious side. It was one of forty-eight national museums chosen for a special program of the American Association of State and Local History.

Ode to a Dead Salmon

"But soft! What splash from yonder stream I hear?"

So opens one of the winning entries from the Ode to a Dead Salmon bad writing contest. During the height of the July salmon run each year, the 49 Alaska Writing Center (645 West Third Avenue, Anchorage) opens this tongue-in-cheek (hook in jaw?) competition to all comers. The idea is to write the best bad Alaskan poetry or prose, with the winner to be decided by a vote of the readers at www.49writers .blogspot.com after an esteemed panel of judges narrows the field from the haikued, limericked, politicized, hard-boiled, and country-balladed entries.

The idea for the contest came indirectly from the late John Haines, one of Alaska's most loved writers, who wrote in *The Writer as Alaskan* about newcomers who kept mining the same literary territory, producing "odes to dead salmon" again and again.

Deciding that an annual purging would be the best cure for this literary ailment, 49 Writers launched the Ode to a Dead Salmon contest in 2009 and has been attracting a virtual freezer-full of fishy entries ever since.

Beyond this funny business, the 49 Alaska Writing Center (www.49writingcenter.org) offers programming and events to support Alaska writers and their work.

★ ★

Off-Road Politicians
Juneau

Out of sight, out of mind, off the road. From the remote location of our state's capital, you'd think that's how Alaskans prefer their government.

When the Russians set up their capital in Sitka during the eighteenth century, no one worried about roads. The Russians did their travel and trading by water. Even when the territorial capital moved from Sitka to Juneau in 1906, Alaska's road system—such as it is—was not much more than a far-away dream. The tent city that would grow into Anchorage, now surpassing Juneau in population nearly ten times over, was on nobody's radar.

The Alaska Railroad, commissioned by President Wilson, made a boom town of Anchorage. Eventually all roads converged there—the Seward Highway coming north off the Kenai, the Glenn bringing traffic from Fairbanks and Valdez via the Richardson Highway, and the Parks running north past Denali to Fairbanks. But not one of these roads comes within five hundred miles of Juneau.

Juneau's not only off the modern-day road system—it's also darned hard to fly into. It's flanked by mountains on one side and ocean on the other; during the late winter months of the legislative season, the weather has an annoying habit of socking in hard.

Over the objections of Juneauites, Alaskans have voted more than once on measures to move the capital from Juneau. Locked in a long-time rivalry with the state's largest city, Fairbanks residents fought efforts to move the state capital to Anchorage, though many government offices are already situated there.

Once an initiative passed that would have moved the capital to the sleepy little town of Willow, a compromise spot seventy miles north of Anchorage and 280 miles south of Fairbanks. Land speculation near Willow went wild. But voters failed to fund the move, so Alaska's distinction of having the only off-road capital city continues.

A grizzly guards the Alaska state
capitol building in Juneau.
PHOTO BY G. M. FERENCY

Traveling Campground

You won't find some of Alaska's best-loved campgrounds on any state maps. That's because they're aboard the MV *Kennicott,* the MV *LeConte,* the MV *Malaspina,* the MV *Tustemena,* and the rest of the big boats that travel the Alaska Marine Highway System.

Commonly known as the Alaska state ferry, the Alaska Marine Highway fleet includes eleven vessels that cover four different routes. The most trafficked route is along the beautiful Inside Passage, with connecting service via the Cross Gulf route to Southwest Alaska and the Aleutians.

You can rent cabins on most of the ferries, but if you're looking to save some money and enjoy a unique camping experience, you're also welcome to pitch your tent on the top deck. If that's a tad too adventurous for your style, travelers are also allowed to sleep under the covered solariums and in the passenger lounge's recliners. All you need is a sleeping bag. For details visit www.dot.state.ak.us/amhs.

The MV *Malsapina,* one of eleven vessels that travel the Alaska Marine Highway System
PHOTO BY G. M. FERENCY

★ ★

Black Wolf of the Glacier

Juneau

As Alaska's state capital, Juneau has seen its share of notorious characters. Wyatt Earp passed through in 1900 on his way to the goldfields of Nome. Our own state legislators kept the FBI busy for years, running surveillance on their alleged misdeeds with Big Oil. And then there's a certain former governor who abandoned her post midterm after a rock-star launch in the 2008 presidential election.

Romeo, the black wolf who interacted with humans and dogs near Juneau's Mendenhall Glacier.
PHOTO BY SETH KANTNER, KAPVIK PHOTOGRAPHY

★ ★

At least as famous as these, and more popular with many of the town's residents, was Juneau's celebrity wolf. As their love affair grew, people began calling him Romeo. Romeo was first spotted near Juneau's Mendenhall Glacier in 2003, when he won over the hearts of Juneau residents by posing for photos, joining their hikes, and socializing with their dogs. He took to hanging out by the West Glacier trailhead, and he treated most of the humans and pets who came through there as part of his pack.

There was speculation that Romeo might have lost his mate in an accident, though no one knew for certain why this particular wolf lived alone. Concerned that he might become too accustomed to people for his own good, wildlife officials at one point threatened to move him, but there were so many objections that they settled for signs reminding visitors to the Mendenhall area to treat the wolf with respect.

Romeo would often be seen sunning himself on large rocks, erratics left by the glacier. He might appear in the woods as if out of nowhere, sometimes nudging a hand or a leg for attention. It was once reported he ran off with a small dog in his mouth but released it unharmed after only a moment.

Sadly, Juneau's love affair with its wolf ended tragically. Romeo disappeared in the fall of 2009. There were hopes he'd run off with a new love of his own kind, but in fact a poacher was apprehended with a black wolf hide that bore markings unique to the black wolf of the glacier.

Unspeakable Acts Research Centre
Juneau

A few blocks from the Governor's Mansion in Juneau, at the corner of Seventh and Franklin—where Franklin isn't a real street but rather a set of stairs directing pedestrians down one of Juneau's steep hills—you'll stumble upon what looks like an old white garage. But it's no garage: It's the Unspeakable Acts Research Centre.

16

★ ★

No one's saying exactly what goes on inside the Unspeakable Acts Research Centre in Juneau.
PHOTO BY B. B. MACKENZIE

What sort of unspeakable acts are studied behind the big double doors? No one's saying for certain. But we do know that the center is the brainchild of William Spear, who once chaired the board of a big venture-capital bank but who, for the past three decades, has built a business of handcrafting enamel pins.

It might seem an odd swap, but for Spear it's a matter of proving that you can do what you love and still make a living. He designs and sells hundreds of pins and zipper pulls from his shop, Wm. Spear Designs, on the real Franklin Street. Each is the result of a laborious

★ ★

process that begins with copper shapes punched from an engraved die. Glass-based enamels colored with metal oxides are applied with a tiny brush or syringe. Due to different melting points, each color is applied separately.

Since there's no open admission to the Unspeakable Acts Research Centre, the best we can do is recommend you visit Spear's website (www.wmspear.com), where by clicking on buttons like "Fun" you'll see not just his trademark Running Mummy enamel but also a short animated film featuring thirteen enamel figures, including a habañero and a DNA helix.

Spear's not just making pins. He calls them "talismans, amulets, and charms for an uncertain world." And if research into unspeakable acts helps him to do it, who are we to protest?

Baranof Suite 604
Juneau

From the raucous days of the gold rush to cash that flowed free and easy when Alaska's oil pipeline was under construction, our hotels hosted more than a few unsavory deals. Among the most recent are the activities that went on in the now infamous Suite 604 of the Baranof Hotel, only blocks from the state capitol building.

A classy, historic downtown hotel, the Baranof was previously known for its art deco lobby and artwork by prominent Alaska artists like Sydney Lawrence and Eustace Zeiglar. Then the oil service company Veco rented Suite 604 during the 2006 legislative session, and unbeknownst to the legislators who stopped by to talk with Bill Allen, Veco's chief executive, the room was under FBI surveillance. Video footage shows cash being passed and favors discussed. Arrests and indictments ensued, with charges of corruption leveled against several legislators.

A few traded the comforts of Suite 604 for a sobering penance served behind bars. Then things got complicated. Some of the federal prosecutors also landed in hot water, leading to a storm of appeals.

The door to one of Juneau's most infamous—
and now most-requested—hotel rooms
PHOTO BY B. B. MACKENZIE

★ ★

During the same session that gave Suite 604 its reputation, a newspaper piece named eleven legislators who'd allegedly received large campaign contributions from Veco. Reportedly some bar talk about these "corrupt bastards" led to the loosely formed Corrupt Bastards Club, with its members—all state legislators—sporting CBC ball caps to poke fun at their own reputations.

Suite 604 is quieter now. But the Baranof still gets requests for the room from guests who want to stay where all the action was.

Four-Legged Welcome
Juneau

For years, visitors to Juneau could get there only by ship. And when boats pulled in to dock, they were met by the four friendly paws and the wagging tail of Patsy Ann, a bull terrier proclaimed by the mayor to be the city's official greeter.

No one ever told Patsy Ann when the ships would be in. Somehow she knew on her own, and she never missed one. It wasn't the blasts from their horns that alerted her—Patsy Ann was deaf from birth.

Her instincts about arriving ships were keen. One day a crowd gathered at a dock to greet an incoming boat. Patsy Ann joined them at first, but then dashed to another dock. Sure enough, that's where the ship finally pulled in.

Born in Oregon, Patsy Ann arrived in Juneau as a pup. She had no one owner, lodging mostly at the longshoremen's quarters near the town's docks. She wandered freely into saloons and hotel lobbies, and she was as photographed as celebrity dogs from the movies.

As for food, Patsy Ann never lacked. All around town people fed her, including chefs from the cruise ships. Her diet was indulgent, including a daily candy bar, and as she put on pounds, her rush to the docks wasn't quite as vigorous as it once had been.

Patsy Ann passed on in 1942. A crowd turned out at the waterfront to pay their respects as her coffin was lowered into the water. Touched by the story of the faithful white bull terrier, sculptor Anna

**Deaf and homeless, Patsy Ann met
every ship that docked in Juneau.**
ALASKA STATE LIBRARY, BUTLER/DALE COLLECTION, P306-0337

★ ★

Burke Harris of New Mexico cast a bronze statue of Patsy Ann. In 1992, the statue found a home on one of Juneau's main docks, where it perpetually waits for the ships to come in.

Ghost of the Alaskan Hotel
Juneau

Among the most pervasive ghost stories in Alaska is the tale of the ghost of Juneau's Alaskan Hotel at 167 South Franklin Street.

Dating to 1913, the Alaskan is Juneau's oldest hotel in continuous service. At one time it housed a bordello, and as legend has it, the ghost that haunts room 219 was a woman driven to prostitution when her husband didn't return from a mining expedition. But according to legend, the man did eventually show up, and he killed her in anger over what she had done.

Most Juneau residents have heard of the ghost. Some call her Alice. Guests sometimes report seeing people dressed in old-fashioned garb in the hallways, and room 219 is said to often be unnaturally cold. Hotel clerks have had to move guests who feel uneasy there, though there are others who purposely request the room, hoping to have a firsthand encounter with Juneau's most famous ghost.

Checked but Never Claimed
Juneau

Alaska is known as the Last Frontier, so it's not surprising that a Wild West gunslinger made his way north. What's curious, though, is that he left his weapon behind.

Wyatt Earp and his wife, Josephine, left Arizona for Alaska in the crazed rush for Klondike gold. They passed through Juneau on June 27, 1900, and being a lawman himself, Earp obligingly checked his gun with the US marshal upon his arrival. However, he failed to claim it before his steamer, the SS *Senator,* set sail two days later at 5 a.m., a wee bit early for the marshal's office to be open for business.

★ ★

C-H-E-C-K-E-D
BUT NEVER CLAIMED

THIS WEAPON WAS CHECKED AT THE U.S.
MARSHALL'S OFFICE IN JUNEAU, JUNE 27, 1900
BY THE NOTORIOUS GUNFIGHTER
WYATT EARP
EARP DEPARTED FOR NOME ABOARD THE S.S.
SENATOR AT 5:00 A.M. ON JUNE 29th, PRIOR TO THE
OPENING OF THE MARSHALL'S OFFICE

**Wyatt Earp's revolver, checked but never claimed, at
Juneau's Red Dog Saloon**
PHOTO BY G. M. FERENCY

No one knows for certain how Earp's gun found its way from the marshal to the Red Dog Saloon, but there are rumors it was given up as a prize in a poker game. Distinguished by its lack of a trigger guard, the gun now hangs in a glass case behind the bar at the Red Dog (278 South Franklin Street).

As for the Earps, they operated a canteen in Saint Michael at the mouth of the Yukon River, where they apparently landed too late to make the trip to Dawson City before freeze-up. Tex Rickard, the famed

★ ★

promoter who later built Madison Square Garden, convinced them there was more money to be made in nearby Nome anyhow, since most of the Klondike was already staked

Even without his weapon, Earp made a big splash in Nome. With a partner, he built the Dexter Saloon, the largest establishment of its kind in a town that had plenty of watering holes. The Dexter was the first two-story wooden structure in town, with twelve club rooms upstairs

Outlaws, Rebels, and Cons

You have to give this place credit: We're one of the youngest states in the Union, and already we're on our third edition of playing cards featuring outlaws, rebels, and cons.

It's not every state that can stack the deck with fifty-two notorious characters. Our advantage comes from the fiery independent spirit with which the frontier was—sort of—tamed. It's that fuzzy line between doing whatever you please and breaking the law that fills out the card deck. Plus Alaska's a good faraway place for folks on the lam to hide out.

Featured in the new edition of the Alaska Outlaw playing cards are Soapy Smith (see page 137), Sarah Palin, Steve McQueen, and Levi Johnston. Each card features a photo and an explanation of the questionable or nefarious activity that landed the character a place in the deck. You'll find the cards at Alaska gift shops and at www.alaskaoutlawcards.com.

where men could enjoy the company of Nome's "working women." Wyatt and Josie left Nome in the fall of 1901, purportedly with a small fortune of $80,000. A fire later leveled nearly every building on Front Street, including the Dexter.

Though separated from his revolver in Juneau, Earp was rarely at a loss for a weapon. After leaving Alaska, he reportedly joined Virgil Earp in avenging the death of their brother.

Alaska's outlaws, rebels, and cons may have dealt the state a bad hand, but they also give us plenty to talk about.
PHOTO BY B. B. MACKENZIE

★ ★

Commissioner of Mirth

Juneau

What's so funny about Alaska? Quite a lot, if you ask fast-talking Jeff Brown, Juneau's jack of all trades and comedian extraordinaire. Brown holds certificates, all issued by various Alaskan governors, proclaiming him Alaska's Commissioner of Mirth, Minister of Merriment, and Professor of Play.

A local icon and DJ at Juneau's KTOO radio, Brown came to Alaska from California in 1975 and set right to his funny business. He began

Jeff Brown, Alaska's Commissioner of Mirth, at one of his favorite fishing holes
PHOTO BY JEFF BROWN

with an annual April Fools' "news" publication called the *Juneau What*. Falling as it does in the midst of Alaska's legislative session, April Fools' Day was just too nice an opportunity for Brown to pass up.

After printing the *What* for nearly two decades, Brown has switched up to a full-color magazine called *Real Alaskan*. It's anyone's guess what's real and not between the slick covers. The how-to article "Cleaning the Mendenhall Glacier" involves a real vacuum cleaner on a real glacier, but we're not claiming the beast will pass a white-glove inspection anytime soon.

In addition to digging up funny stuff about the forty-ninth state, Brown performs as a magician, balloon artist, and member of a local comedy troupe. His magazine can be found at local booksellers.

Bridge to Nowhere

Ketchikan

Think back to your last trip to the airport: the traffic, the parking garages, the taxis queued up for fares. And then there's the waiting. The towns change, but the routine stays the same.

Unless you're flying from Ketchikan. The last time I left there, I watched three killer whales surface, black fins gleaming, as they swam between the airport and me. That's because between the airport on Gravina Island and the city of Ketchikan, there's only ocean, so part of the trip involves riding a ferry from the city to the airport—and if you're lucky, some whales.

Everybody may love whales, but a lot of people in Ketchikan would just as soon drive a bridge to get to the airport. Enter Rep. Don Young and the late senator Ted Stevens, who pushed for federal funding to build a structure taller than the Brooklyn Bridge—to accommodate cruise ships traveling beneath it—and almost as long as San Francisco's Golden Gate Bridge. The price tag? A whopping $398 million.

The Bridge to Nowhere, as the Gravina Island Bridge came to be called, soon became a miscreant poster child for pork barrel spending. It wasn't a claim to fame that Ketchikan especially wanted, but there

★ ★

With the Bridge to Nowhere unfunded, a ferry transports passengers between Ketchikan and the airport on Gravina Island.
PHOTO BY B. B. MACKENZIE

wasn't much they could do to about it, aside from flaunting T-shirts that read "Nowhere, Alaska, 99901."

In 2005, Congress axed the federal earmark, so Ketchikan continues to rely on ferries to transport passengers to and from the airport. But funding for the Gravina Island road to the bridge was already in place, so now there's a $25 million dollar Gravina Island Highway that dead-ends where the bridge would have been.

★ ★

The Gravina Island Bridge project is all but dead now. A proposed Knik Arm project connecting Anchorage to Knik Road and Wasilla is the state's new controversial "bridge to nowhere." The 2.7-mile toll bridge, last penciled at $700 million, is still under discussion.

Married Man's Trail
Ketchikan

First there's the aisle. Then there's the trail. That's how it went, anyhow, for the married men of Ketchikan, back in the days when the Creek District brothels were active.

Today there's a street sign that gives up the secret, marking the boardwalk that follows the creek through a dark swath of forest—the route the town's respectable men used when sneaking a visit to the Creek District "sporting girls."

The history of this infamous path through the woods began in 1903, when it was determined that the town would be better off if bawdy houses were gathered in one place. Early maps designated these houses of ill repute with the initials *F. B.,* standing for "Female Boarders," a euphemism for prostitutes.

Unlike the tiny one-room cribs where these illicit activities were conducted in Fairbanks, Dawson City, and Juneau, the houses on Creek Street were lively party spots. When the fishing boats were in port, the Creek District hosted a good share of fighting and brawling and carrying on. Sanitation was poor; at low tide, you could see where sewage was dumped in the creek, which thankfully flowed fast enough to expel it into the ocean before the smell got too awful. Occasionally a floater—a corpse from a party gone bad—would turn up near the mouth of the creek.

Cash flowed as fast as the water, in and out of the District. When things got too rowdy, the police ran raids, which were inevitably followed by "tributes" to ensure the doors to the brothels stayed open. Though confined to their own part of town, the working girls weren't known to be shy, whistling to tourists and showing their bared legs.

★ ★

**Street sign for Married Man's Trail, once a
clandestine route, now a major attraction**
PHOTO BY B. B. MACKENZIE

Every so often the city officials would proclaim that the District's
illicit activities had gotten entirely out of hand. They'd shut down the
brothels, and traffic on Married Man's Trail would fall off. In 1954,
Ketchikan outlawed brothels for good. A few of the working women
stayed on at their old properties, with the last of them passing on in
the mid-1970s. Today Married Man's Trail still runs from the top of the
hill to the Creek District, but there's no sneaking required. The shops
at the Creek—bookstores and galleries and restaurants—sell nothing
to get a husband in trouble.

✱ ✱

Troll Art
Ketchikan

Ketchikan's got its own Troll. Not the kind that lives under a bridge, though his shop is conveniently located near one, but Ray Troll, whose unique brand of fish art has made a big—ahem—splash.

Troll art inspires the waking of the dead, as proclaimed on a T-shirt promoting a Raven's Brew blend, coffee originally roasted in Ketchikan.
PHOTO BY B. B. MACKENZIE

31

★ ★

From "The Baitful Dead" to "Embrace Your Inner Fish" to "Humpies from Hell" to "Wild King: You Make My Heart Sing," Troll's got a seemingly endless supply of funny fish puns to go with his art. They're featured on T-shirts and ball caps, posters and coasters, playing cards and coffee mugs, plus a slew of other products. He also designs logos for Raven's Brew Coffee, a venture that started in Ketchikan before expanding to Anchorage and Washington State.

Troll came to Alaska in 1983 to help his sister start a seafood shop. Leaving dead fish for live art, he says he has been "featuring the slightly inappropriate" since 1985. Today Troll and his wife run Soho Coho, a gallery and gift shop housed in a former brothel in Ketchikan's Creek District, at the bottom of Married Man's Trail (see previous entry).

Much of Troll's art is funny, but to some there's a serious side. Drawing from fossils of prehistoric fish, he created a unique blend of science and art that found its way into museums and bookstores, capturing several distinctive awards. Troll's touring shows include Dancing to the Fossil Record; Sharkabet: A Sea of Sharks from A to Z; and Cruisin' the Fossil Freeway. He's even got enough clout to have a New Zealand fish named for him—a ratfish, of course.

Featuring vibrant colors and eye-catching designs, there's nothing haughty about Troll's quirky creations, yet he has lectured at Ivy League schools, and his work has gone on display at the Smithsonian. He also plays in a local band, the Ratfish Wranglers, making good on his claim that "everyone should be in a band regardless of talent or ambition." Troll's Soho Coho Gallery is at 5 Creek Street in Ketchikan, in the historic Star Building.

Alaska Men

Let's get a few things straight about Alaska's men. First, there's the persistent notion that they vastly outnumber the women up here. While that was true in the past, these days the state's population is almost evenly divided between women and men. But old notions die hard, and it will likely be a long time before folks up here quit talking about how the "odds are good, but the goods are odd" when it comes to Alaska's men. Alas, there are no census statistics we can reference to disprove the second half of the saying.

Then there are those bumper stickers proclaiming ALASKA: WHERE MEN ARE MEN, AND WHERE WOMEN WIN THE IDITAROD. Alaska's men can thank Libby Riddles for that one. She and her dogs took first place in the 1985 Iditarod Sled Dog Race, to be followed by multiple wins by Iditarod legend Susan Butcher.

Alaska's men do have one up on women in one department, however: They've got their own magazine. The *AlaskaMen* magazine (www.alaskamen.com) is the brainchild of Anchorage resident Susie Carter, self-proclaimed matchmaker and promoter of Alaska's finest men. Capitalizing on the stereotype of the rugged but lonely wilderness guy, Carter began her full-color magazine in 1985, featuring Alaska bachelors and inviting women to correspond with the hunks of their dreams—after checking the "taken list," of course. The magazine got top billing on quite a few national television shows, and it's still going strong. No word on the exact marriage stats that have come from the effort.

Forever Bronzed
Ketchikan

Proud moms used to get their baby's shoes bronzed. So why not memorialize a town's proud history by bronzing its artifacts? That's the concept that led Ketchikan artist Dave Rubin and his sister Judy to fashion "the Rock," a bronzed rendering of Ketchikan's history placed front and center along the waterfront's Berth I.

The Rock depicts seven types of people who contributed to the community of Ketchikan: a Tlingit chief, a miner, a logger, a

Along the Ketchikan waterfront, residents past— and present—are immortalized in the Rock.
PHOTO BY B. B. MACKENZIE

fisherman, a native woman, a pioneer woman, and an aviator. As models for each historical figure, the Rubins enlisted prominent contemporary citizens of their town. Nathan Jackson, the famed local carver of totem poles, posed for Tlingit Chief Johnson. Thrust into the energetic role of a pioneer woman is Hilary Koch, one of the original founders of Raven's Brew ("Wake the Dead") coffee.

Others contributed artifacts to be preserved forever in bronze. The native woman, for instance, wears a woven cedar hat made by a local craftsperson, Grace DeWitt, and given to the mother of Irene Dundas, who posed for the woman. Others donated XtraTuff boots for the fisherman and logger's pants (cut off near the knee so they wouldn't get caught in machinery). To tourists, it's history; to Ketchikan residents, the Rock feels like home.

Waves of Disaster

Lituya Bay

Lituya is one of the quiet, picturesque bays that grace Southeast Alaska. But don't be fooled by its picturesque presence. Lituya has a tumultuous past.

One problem arises from the bay's narrow mouth. It's only a third of a mile across, with a navigable channel that's even more narrow, though the bay itself is nine miles long and two miles wide. The result is both strong tidal currents and treacherous tsunami conditions. In 1786, one of the first Europeans to explore the bay, Jean-Francois de la Parouse, lost twenty-one of his crew to the sweeping tide. Nearly two centuries later, in 1958, an earthquake at nearby Crillon Island triggered a massive tsunami that felled huge trees high in the mountains and stripped the earth down to the bedrock. Of three fishing boats in the bay at the time, two somehow managed to survive the wave.

But Lituya Bay's history of disaster goes beyond natural phenomena to a chilling tale of cabin fever gone horribly wrong. In 1897, a married couple named Hans and Edith Nelson joined thousands of

**As seen from the air, the narrow mouth of Lituya Bay
makes it especially treacherous.**
ALASKA STATE LIBRARY PHOTOGRAPH COLLECTION, P01-3334

prospectors in the rush for Klondike gold. Disappointed by logistical challenges and slim prospects, they opted out of the Klondike and, with three other prospectors, were transported by canoe to Lituya Bay.

The summer yielded a fair amount of gold, though it was no fortune when divided by five. Then winter set in, trapping all five in a three-room cabin. One morning, Michael Dennin, the fun-loving but anger-prone Irishman of the bunch, shot two of the men in cold blood at the breakfast table.

Hans and Edith managed to wrestle Dennin to the ground. They bound him and set about trying to decide what to do with him. Standing twenty-four-hour guard required more stamina than they could muster

★ ★

between them, so they held court. Edith and Hans served as both judge and jury, with local Indians recruited to witness Dennin's confession. The couple then turned executioners, hanging Dennin for his crime.

That's more or less how Jack London told it in his story "The Unexpected," published by *McClure's Magazine* in 1909. Skagway pioneer M. B. Keller claimed London's account was true. A more recent fictionalized version of the tale is Lynn D'Urso's *Heartbroke Bay*.

Devil's Country
Petersburg

Among the stories that rushed from Alaska and the Klondike along with the gold, tales of hidden valleys and treasures were especially popular. Among the most lasting was a mysterious tale recorded by Harry D. Colp in a pamphlet called *The Strangest Story Ever Told* that still circulates in the Petersburg area.

Colp tells of how in 1900 he and his friends Charlie, Fred, and John decided they'd try to locate the source of a quartz rock richly veined with gold. Acquired from a local Indian, the rock was said to have come from a lake shaped like a half moon that was tucked in some desolate country up the Patterson River from Thomas Bay, also called the Bay of Death, due to a large landslide.

Trip after trip was made into the region of the half-moon lake, which Colp took to calling the Devil's Country. Charlie came back from the first journey claiming devilish creatures covered in hair and reeking with sores had chased him to his canoe. He left Alaska, vowing never to return.

John and Fred were the next to go in. Like Charlie, Fred took the first boat he could catch out of the country, petrified of a creature that he claimed had hitched a ride on the bow of his canoe. John told a different version, saying he'd come upon Fred in the woods, barking like a dog and crawling around on all fours, pulling up pine saplings. John and Colp made the third trip to Devil's country, where nighttime scratching and scrambling sent them scurrying home.

★ ★

Convinced that there was gold to be had and curious about what was really going on back by the lake, Colp returned with Mr. Bush, a big bartender who described the country as it had appeared to him in a dream. On the trek back toward the lake, Bush reportedly fell, hitting his head. When he came to, he accused Colp of trying to hurt him and insisted the river was flowing away from the ocean instead of toward it.

Not one to give up, Colp returned to the Devil's Country in 1911 with a Norwegian man who returned from washing up at the lake saying he didn't feel well and needed to get out. When they got back to town, he told everyone they'd prospected for two weeks when in fact they'd done no such thing. Prospectors returning from the area in 1914 and 1919 told conflicting stories, agreeing on nothing except that they would never go back. In 1925, a trapper found tracks in the snow that seemed a cross between a small bear's and a small barefoot human's. He returned to investigate and was never heard from again.

Fact or fiction? Harry Colp is gone now, and we'll likely never know. But the stories he told of the strange things that went on in the Devil's Country continue to amuse and amaze.

Valhalla
Petersburg

In the quaint fishing town of Petersburg along the Inside Passage, Alaska has its own Little Norway, complete with a replica of a Viking ship.

Noting the fishing potential in this part of Alaska (halibut, herring, salmon, shrimp, crab) Norwegian settlers passed on the usual mining and logging enterprises when they founded this picturesque town. Though Petersburg now has some three thousand residents, big cruise ships can't get from Wrangell Narrows into the town's narrow harbor, so the community remains quiet and unspoiled even during the busy summer tourist season.

In celebration of its heritage, rosemaling decorates downtown Petersburg shops, and a troupe of young dancers performs to folk

★ ★

The *Valhalla*, Alaska's lone Viking ship, near
Hammer Slough in the fishing town of Petersburg,
also known as the state's Little Norway
PHOTO BY G. M. FERENCY

music in the Sons of Norway Hall. Near Hammer Slough, a Viking ship
in the seaside Fisherman's Park looks poised to set sail.

During the third weekend in May when the town celebrates Norwegian Independence Day with a Little Norway Festival, Viking raids
are staged from the square-sailed replica, christened the *Valhalla*. The
ship was reportedly purchased by the city of Petersburg in 1976, two
years after it was built. Also in the park is a memorial to fishermen lost
at sea. From the park's deck, look up, and you're likely to see a bald
eagle or two, keeping watch over the *Valhalla*.

★ ★

Humpy 500
Petersburg

What do you do to get kids excited about a seafood festival? Add go-karts, of course. In the scenic Norwegian-style fishing town of Petersburg in Southeast Alaska, the go-kart competition, dubbed the Humpy 500, has outlasted the festival it was originally linked with.

Held each fall after commercial fishing winds down, the Humpy 500 celebrates the end of the season with local children from grades two through seven building their own go-karts and racing them through the streets of Petersburg. Oil drums are used for the bodies, with wheels, roll bars, and brakes attached for propulsion and safety. To help the kids put it all together, the cannery opens its machine shop to the community prior to the start of the race.

Themes tend toward the fishy, with prizes awarded not only for speed but for best costumes and the most original carts. Past winners include go-karts named Silver Swordfish, Red October, Salmon Wars, and Black Cod Pearl.

Older than Your Average Bear
Prince of Wales Island

Twelve thousand years old, give or take a few years—that's the age of the brown bear skeleton discovered in 1990 at the El Capitan Cave on Prince of Wales Island in Southeast Alaska.

Although you might not think of Alaska as prime spelunking country, there are actually several caves on Prince of Wales Island. With more than thirteen thousand feet of passageways, El Capitan is the largest in the state and one of the biggest mapped caves in North America. The limestone in these caves indicates that the island broke off from the South Pacific plate and moved north millions of years ago.

Riddled with puncture and bite marks from another bear, the huge brown bear skeleton was discovered near a complete black bear skeleton dating over ten thousand years old. Both Pleistocene bears were much larger than modern bears. Discovery of the skeletons has changed

* *

**Exploring El Capitan Cave on Prince of Wales
Island is not for the timid.**
PHOTO BY B. B. MACKENZIE

thinking about where the Ice Age extended and the range of bears.
There are no brown bears on Prince of Wales Island today, or on any
island south of Frederick Sound for that matter. It was once thought this
had to do with the presence of black bears on the islands to the south,
but the El Capitan discoveries have scientists rethinking that theory.

In the summer, you can take a free guided tour of El Capitan Cave,
courtesy of the Thorne Bay Ranger District of the US Forest Service. From

★ ★

mainland Alaska, you can access the island by boat or floatplane. The cave site is approximately three hours by road from Thorne Bay. Expect conditions that are apparently just right for the average bear: a steep hike to the cave, no trails or lighting inside, wet mud, and a chilly interior temperature that helped preserve the bear's skeletal remains.

Sitka Cemeteries
Sitka

Stroll through the former capital of Russian America and you'll not only run into some of its friendly residents, you'll also stumble onto the final resting places of a few who've passed on.

Three little cemeteries are hidden away on a hill at the end of Observatory Street, right in the middle of town. They're so mossy and dark that you may find yourself listening for the sound of pounding hooves from Washington Irving's spooky tale. Accessible only by trail, these graves date from the nineteenth century into the twenty-first century. In much of the hollow, the rain forest has had its way with the crooked cement and wooden markers. Russian Orthodox crosses, distinguished by parallel diagonal lines slashing a vertical post, top several of the graves.

On a nearby hill where a reconstructed Russian blockhouse overlooks the harbor, there are three more gravesites, all with markers inscribed in Russian. One tops the burial site of a Russian princess. The year of her death was 1748.

A few blocks away, off Jeff Davis Street, is the Sitka National Cemetery, with rows of white slab markers. Farther from town, down Indian River Road, there are still more gravesites tucked in the woods, a sad reminder of the aftereffects of colonialism, when Native Alaskans shipped to Sitka to be treated for tuberculosis succumbed to the disease, far from family and home.

Near a replica of Sitka's Russian blockhouse lies
the final resting place of a Russian princess, one of
many gravesites tucked into a downtown hill.

★ ★

Secret Sanctuary
Sitka

Steeples, bells, stained glass—those are some of the signs of a church. But in Sitka's Russian Bishop's House, there's a beautiful little chapel with no steeple, no bell, and no stained glass. In fact it's not a separate building at all—the chapel is tucked on the second floor of the meticulously restored painted log building now known as the Russian Bishop's House.

One of the few standing buildings from Russian Alaska, the Russian Bishop's House was built in 1842. The bishops who lived there had charge of Orthodox parishioners from eastern Siberia through the Aleutians and down the Alaskan coast to California, and their quarters included a religious school downstairs and an ornate chapel upstairs.

By 1969, the house had fallen into such disrepair that the Russian Orthodox Church let it go, but after a sixteen-year effort, the National Park Service has restored the property to its mid-nineteenth-century condition. Now part of Sitka National Historical Park, among the meticulously renovated portions of the house is the Chapel of the Annunciation, filled with glorious icons of religious figures. This quiet, elegant space is an unexpected gem within the large but almost military-looking building. (Formally, it's Russian Colonial style.) The best-known official who lived in the house and worshipped in the private chapel was Bishop Innocent, who was a linguist, a scientist, and a teacher in addition to his clerical role.

Every thirty minutes from 9 a.m. to 5 p.m. during the summer, rangers lead tours of the Russian Bishop's House, including the secret sanctuary, at 201 College Drive.

Filled with beautifully rendered icons, the upstairs
chapel in the Russian Bishop's House is a surprise.
PHOTO BY B. B. MACKENZIE

★ ★

Second Chance Bears
Sitka

The concrete tanks were once used for processing pulp at a local mill. Now they hold bears.

The tanks aren't tiny: Both are 190 feet in diameter, while one is fourteen and one is seventeen feet deep. Transformed into bear habitat, the tanks are giving orphaned bears a second chance.

From outside, the cement tanks are nothing special to look at. At first there were questions about whether the bears might end up used only for the entertainment of tourists, and whether they would be well nourished and exercised. But since it opened in 2007, Sitka's nonprofit Fortress of the Bears has earned the respect of its skeptics. Inside the tank that is currently in use, the orphaned bears scamper and interact much as they would in the wild.

Chaik and Killisnoo, the first pair of orphaned bears to live at the Fortress, came as cubs after their mother learned to look to humans for food because of unsecured trash and was shot at a lodge in Angoon. Often cubs are shot with the mother because without her they cannot survive. But these two got lucky: They were placed at the Fortress, where they grew large, with healthy coats and care that even included some recent dental work for Killisnoo. How do you fix a bear's teeth, you may wonder. Very quickly, it turns out, while the bear is knocked out for spaying.

Some bears brought to the Fortress are eventually placed in zoos. Others find a permanent home there, where visitors have a chance to see bears close up in habitat that, aside from the cement, mimics what they'd find in the wild. The Fortress has its own interpretive expert, and it also facilitates research on bears.

★ ★

Running of the Boots

Sitka

Fishing. Barbecues. Long sunlit days. Those generous tourists only too willing to pull out their plastic to nudge Alaska's economy away from its dependence on oil.

No one likes to see our glorious summers draw to a close, but in true Alaskan spirit, the people of Sitka celebrate summer's end with an annual Running of the Boots, a foot race run in "Sitka sneakers," the local slang for Xtratufs, sturdy knee-high boots that trump all other footwear in Southeast Alaska.

Xtratufs are a big deal in Alaska, especially in Southeast, where you're more likely to be out in the rain or sloshing around in a boat than to worry about making a fashion statement. Made from neoprene, Xtratufs have chevron soles that help prevent slipping on docks. Fish oils can eat through plain rubber boots, but not Xtratufs. All in all, they're a practical if not speedy choice in Southeast Alaska footwear.

Though the company has changed hands a few times, the boots have been around since 1950, and Alaska accounts for approximately one-third of their sales. Larry Johansen of Douglas, near Juneau, has even released a book celebrating the footwear: *Xtratuf: An Alaskan Way of Life.*

The Running of the Boots is about fun rather than speed, though there is a prize category for the fastest boots (and presumably the person wearing them). Prizes are also given for best costume, best couple, and best-dressed boots. Typically the Running of the Boots starts at Crescent Harbor, with contestants opting for either the short loop around Saint Michael's Cathedral in the center of town, or the more competitive route that goes to the intersection of Lincoln and Katlian Streets and back.

And in case you still believe that old saying that there's no such thing as a free lunch, the Running of the Boots aims to disprove it. After the race, contestants are invited to a luncheon hosted by the Alaska Cruise Association. Proceeds from the event go to benefit local charities such as the Sitka Local Foods Network Project.

★ ★

First Defense
Sitka

Watching the seabirds swoop and glide over Sitka's peaceful harbor, you'd never guess that the causeway extending out from the airport once hid guns placed by servicemen from the only Alaskan military base that was operational on December 7, 1941, when the Japanese attacked Pearl Harbor.

Moss-covered concrete bunkers and gun batteries tucked in deep in these forests are now accessible only by water, as overland access would require trespassing over the airport runway, which was constructed as part of the military buildup following the attack on Pearl Harbor. Shrouded in trees, an eerie sense of mystery has settled over the abandoned World War II fortifications on what is now known as the Fort Rousseau Causeway.

Sitka was one of three Navy seaplane bases designed for Alaska as part of Plan Orange to protect US interests in the North Pacific even before the Japanese attack. In 1939, when the Sitka base was commissioned, Alaska was still a territory. Once the country was drawn into war, the US Army Coast Artillery Corps scrambled to construct gun batteries at Shoals Point to protect Sitka Sound. In addition to the batteries, radar and target stations were placed on neighboring islands.

Some of the batteries became obsolete before the project was completed, and some of the magazines that housed them were never finished, adding to the intrigue that surrounds the causeway, which is being developed into a state historical park. Rumors persist that the magazine for one of the batteries was actually an underground hospital, and there are rumors of a secret submarine base nearby, but the real curiosity is the causeway itself, the secret fortress of the Alaska military.

★ ★

Petroglyph Beach
Wrangell

You might expect to find petroglyphs, the iconic communication left by ancient peoples, on cave walls in the southwestern United States. But in Wrangell, Alaska, there are also petroglyphs pecked into boulders that sit along the ocean shore, just above the high-water mark.

Because it contains the largest number of petroglyphs in Southeast Alaska, this beach is now a state historic park. On the park's boardwalk, there are replicas of some of the drawings displayed so visitors can make rubbings of them.

Not much is known about who made the petroglyphs or what the marks mean, though it's believed the rocks document important events such as wars, treaties, potlatches, and the work of shamans. Some designs, such as the spiral, are also found in places like Chaco Canyon in the southwestern United States, suggesting the connection long assumed between Alaska's indigenous tribes and those of the Southwest, such as the Navajo.

Petroglyph Beach is on Grave Street, only a mile from Wrangell's ferry terminal. A visit is bit like a scavenger hunt—there are over forty petroglyphs scattered over the beach, waiting to be found.

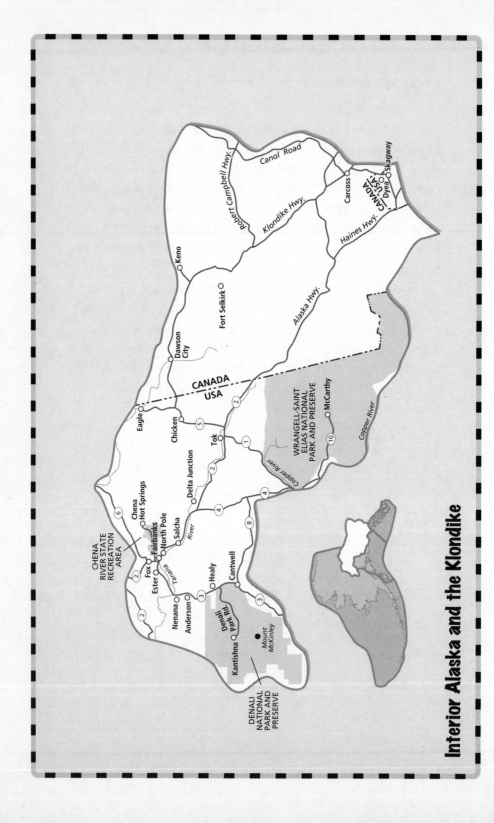

Interior Alaska and the Klondike

2

Interior Alaska and the Klondike

Where's the coldest spot in a place known for cold? Contrary to what you might think, it's not Alaska's North Slope but its Interior. At least that's the case when you consider the coldest winter temperatures, which settle in over the central part of the region, where ocean weather patterns lose their effect. The coldest temperature ever recorded in North America was at Snag, Yukon Territory, on February 3, 1947. On the Alaska side of the border, the temperature that day at Tanacross fell to a bone-chilling seventy-five degrees below zero Fahrenheit.

The cold accounts for quite a few curiosities in Interior Alaska. There are critters with antifreeze—or a substance very much like it—in their bloodstreams, and there's ice fog so thick you can barely see those frostbitten toes. Thanks to the cold, the Interior's dialed directly into the past with well-preserved creatures like Blue Babe, the Ice Age bison. We're even got fire from ice, generated by the highly flammable methane that burps from melting permafrost and also by ice sculpted like a big magnifying glass, concentrating the sun's winter rays.

Unconfirmed but suspected are the effects of the Interior's extreme cold on some of our more curious people. How else to explain a guy who carved his own set of false teeth from bear bones, or the woman who hiked eight hundred miles down the Yukon in 1900—in winter, alone? Or the world-class artists who travel here from all over the world to carve ice like crazy, knowing their masterpieces are destined to melt.

★ ★

There's a certain irreverence here, from glaciers that gallop to the papal red carpet that now covers the floor of a saloon. There are huge stakes set on the movement of ice on the Tanana River each spring, and the winners can drink to their good fortune at Skinny Dick's Halfway Inn, which makes the most of its suggestive name.

Curiosities know no borders, and during the gold rush that spanned from the nineteenth to the twentieth century, prospectors chased their fortunes from Alaska to the Yukon and back to Alaska. So it's only natural that we'd include a few Klondike oddities here, like the famous Sourtoe Cocktails at Dawson City's Downtown Hotel, where your drink comes spiked with a real human toe, and Keno's bottle house, built from beer bottles drained during a frosty winter or two.

★ ★

Land Grab
Anderson

If there's one thing Alaska's got lots of, it's land. Used to be it was more or less free for the taking, and while those opportunities are mostly gone now, every so often there's a chance to grab a parcel the way it was done in the old days.

Lots of our sourdoughs got their start here by homesteading under the federal program established in 1862. Homesteaders could claim up to 160 acres as long as they proved up with a survey, a residence, and a way of supporting themselves from the land. Land in the Mat-Su Valley was transferred to midwestern farmers as part of Roosevelt's New Deal in the 1930s, and after World War II, land was transferred to vets in Soldotna.

When the federal Homestead Act was repealed in 1976, Alaska got a ten-year extension. The state ran its own homesteading program for several years, but today the Department of Natural Resources (www .dnr.alaska.gov) offers land only through periodic sealed-bid sales.

Local needs have put a new twist on the great Alaska land grab. Towns hoping to keep their schools open—the state requires ten students, minimum—have put land up for free, as long as certain requirements are met. A few years ago, high school students in Anderson, north of Denali National Park and Preserve, came up with a plan to save their town after a nearby air force base closed. They proposed the city offer twenty-six one-acre lots free to the first takers.

The land was given first come, first served to hardy folks who camped out in the cold for a shot at the deal. The only catch was a $500 deposit and a promise to build on the lot—at least one thousand square feet, residential—within two years.

Those two years came and went, and although the Anderson land came with platting and power, jobs are hard to come by in this small Interior town, and few of the new landowners have followed through on their good intentions. The Anderson school remains open—for now—but the town hasn't grown as its leaders had hoped.

Alaska's Cool Runnings

You've heard of the Jamaican bobsled team, their Olympic performance immortalized in the Disney film *Cool Runnings*? Less known but no less curious is the Jamaican dogsled team, led by musher Oswald "Newton" Marshall of St. Anne, Jamaica.

An operations manager at Jamaica's Chukka Cove Resort picked the young Marshall to work with three new dogs the resort had acquired to pull sand buggies over the beach. One thing led to another, and in 2005, Newton began mushing dogs in real snow. Two years later, he journeyed north to Whitehorse, Yukon Territory, to train with musher Hans Gott, and in 2009 Newton finished the thousand-mile Yukon Quest Sled Dog Race between Whitehorse and Fairbanks.

After training with four-time Iditarod winner Lance Mackey (see page 96), Newton and his dog team, supported in part by performer Jimmy Buffett, entered the 2010 Iditarod Sled Dog Race. Supporters passed out "Rootin' for Newton" buttons at the Iditarod's ceremonial start in Anchorage, and fans eagerly watched the race boards to see how the enthusiastic Jamaican musher would fare.

The Iditarod requires grit and stamina that's not so essential on the sunny beaches of laid-back Jamaica. But Newton and his dogs prevailed over frostbite and sleep deprivation as they traveled the rugged thousand-plus miles to Nome. Finishing in twelve days, Newton came in forty-seventh out of seventy-one starters, and his dogsled has proven almost as good as the bobsled for putting Jamaica on the map.

Northern Desert

Carcross, Yukon Territory

In the Klondike, you expect soaring mountains, rushing rivers, stalwart glaciers, and rocky moraines. Indeed, Klondike country includes all of that, so majestic it almost makes your eyes hurt. But what you wouldn't expect—and what you'll miss if you blink at the wrong spot on the Klondike Highway—is a desert.

So slow down, keep your eyes peeled, and at kilometer 111 you'll spot the Carcross Desert, 640 acres of fine-grained sand that looks out of place in the rugged northern landscape. It was once billed as the world's smallest desert, but there's rumor that a forty-acre sand patch in Maine has bagged that title.

The Carcross Desert is a series of sand dunes formed from deposits left thousands of years ago when glaciers retreated over a huge lake in the area. The lake dried up, leaving dunes that support plants not common up here, such as Baikal sedge, which is more typically found in Asia. Because less-hardy plants that grow in other parts of the Klondike can't survive in the sand, especially with the strong winds that blow from nearby Lake Bennett, the area remains arid despite its small size.

Because most rain falls on the coastal side of the mountains, this "desert" is indeed drier than neighboring coastal climates, but it's not arid enough to qualify as true desert. Another northern desertlike region, much larger, is found in Alaska's remote Kobuk Valley National Park (see page 248), where the largest dunes in the Arctic were likewise formed out of glacial silt. Attempts have been made to limit activity in the Carcross Desert, but it remains a popular recreation area for local hikers, picnickers, skiers, and snowboarders.

Parrot Grave
Carcross

The Carcross Cemetery is a special place. Three of the four who made the original Klondike gold strike are buried there. But one of the fanciest monuments marks the final resting place of a bird: Polly the Parrot, a well-known bird that for more than fifty years entertained guests at the local hotel with banter and songs.

First called Caribou Crossing because of the herds migrating between Bennett and Tagish Lakes, the Carcross area has been occupied by First Nations people for thousands of years. Among them were those whose Anglo names were Skookum Jim, Tagish Charley, and Kate Carmack. These three Tagish Indians, along with George Carmack, found gold in large quantities near Dawson City, Yukon Territory, sparking the 1898 rush to the Klondike. Caribou Crossing became a favorite stop for stampeders, with a sawmill that built boats needed to navigate the waterways to Dawson.

At first a tent city, Carcross eventually became home to hotels and a restaurant called the Arctic, opened by Fred Trump, grandfather to Donald. Built in 1898, the Caribou Hotel was destroyed in a fire in 1909. Polly, a male parrot, came to live at the reconstructed hotel in 1918 when his owner Capt. James Alexander asked the hotel to look after the bird while he and his wife traveled Outside (to the continental US). The couple died in the wreck of the *Princess Sophia* north of Juneau, and Polly stayed on at the hotel for another fifty-four years, singing opera and shocking some patrons with his profanity.

Having lived to the ripe old age of 126, Polly passed on to parrot heaven in 1972. The funeral was an elaborate affair that began with a luncheon at the Caribou Hotel. After the meal, mourners formed a funeral procession to the cemetery, where Carcross resident Johnnie Johns gave the eulogy and sang Polly's favorite "I Love You Truly" before the coffin was lowered near the cemetery entrance. A collection was taken up for the fine marker that memorializes one of the Yukon's most colorful birds.

★ ★

Because the cemetery is sacred ground, visitors are discouraged. A better stop is the Caribou Hotel, once again undergoing renovation, across from the visitor information center and next to the Matthew Watson General Store.

**The final resting place of Polly the Parrot,
in the Carcross Cemetery**
PHOTO BY G. M. FERENCY

This Place Is Bugged

It's Alaska's unofficial state bird: the pesky mosquito, which shows up in outrageous quantities to spoil our enjoyment of the wilderness. We joke about their size, but except for the slow-moving species that pop up in the spring the way daffodils do other places, ours are really no bigger than anywhere else. They're just ferocious.

We all know that mosquitoes are a vital part of the ecosystem, an important food source for fish in particular, but we're still trying to figure out why the fish can't be content just snapping at the bait we dangle from the ends of our fishing lines.

Another loathsome bug of Alaska is the hornet. These easily provoked meat lovers turn out in droves when the weather in Interior Alaska gets especially sunny and warm. They'll swarm a hot dog in seconds if you're daring enough to attempt a picnic when they're at their peak.

It's not only humans who are bugged by our bugs. Biologists say mosquitoes have been known to suck five pounds of blood out of a single caribou over the course of a summer. Much of the open country that caribou travel is tundra, soggy from the permafrost underneath, the perfect breeding habitat for mosquitoes. To get away from the bugs, a caribou will sometimes lie down on a late-melting patch of snow.

Mosquitoes aren't the only pests plaguing our caribou. In late July, as the mosquitoes have moved past their peak, warble flies hatch on the tundra. Attracted by the carbon dioxide exhaled by large mammals, warble flies like to lay their eggs in a caribou's hair. As the larvae burrow under their skin, the caribou can become so irritated that they'll charge like broncos, heads down and legs bucking.

As if that weren't enough, caribou also have to contend with the nasal bot fly, which lays its eggs in a caribou's nostrils. The bot fly's larvae have been found in golf-ball-sized clumps in a caribou's windpipe.

Thank heavens for winter. Bitter cold, blowing winds, drifting snow. That's what it takes to do in our bugs.

★ ★

Big Dreamer
Chena Hot Springs

Since its beginnings, Alaska has attracted people who dream big. A lot of those dreams never make it out of the box, but among those with a reputation for making the seemingly impossible happen is Bernie Karl, a Fairbanks-area entrepreneur who is turning Chena Hot Springs Resort into a model for green power.

Raised in a family of sixteen children, Karl learned from a young age the importance of being resourceful. He went north to mine gold and eventually landed in a different sort of mineral work, running a scrap metal business near Fairbanks. But he also noticed the undeveloped potential in Chena Hot Springs Resort, a ramshackle collection of cabins and a rather run-down pool built up around a natural hot springs discovered by miners way back in 1905.

First with some skepticism, then with admiration, locals watched Karl transform the place into a destination resort. He added a forty-room hotel, refurbished the pool, built an outdoor soaking pond, and fed the tourist market with a menu of seasonal activities, from dog-sledding in winter to hiking in summer. Winter brings Japanese tourists by the busload, eager to travel sixty miles from Fairbanks to get away from any city lights that would inhibit views of the northern lights.

But those were all ordinary improvements, and Karl is no ordinary guy. He also added an ice hotel, and when it melted the first summer, he built it again. Dismayed by the escalating costs of running his full-fledged resort on diesel fuel, he then teamed up with German engineer Gwen Holdmann to create the state's first geothermal power plant. Experts claimed it couldn't be done—that the 165-degree spring waters weren't hot enough to generate that sort of power. Bernie Karl takes that sort of nay-saying as a challenge. By 2006, the resort was getting not only its heat but also electricity from the springs for which it was named. Nowhere else in the world is geothermal commercial power produced from waters of this temperature.

★ ★

Naturally, Bernie Karl didn't stop there. He found a geothermal system to keep his ice hotel and museum from melting. And he has big hopes of spreading his vision and energy to remote villages struggling to free themselves from the need for diesel generators for power. He's won over the skeptics, proving that with grit, determination, and innovation, big dreams sometimes do come true.

If you want to visit Bernie Karl's innovative improvements, Chena Hot Springs Resort is easy to find: It's at the end of the sixty-mile long Chena Hot Springs Road northeast of Fairbanks.

Ice Bound

Chena Hot Springs

Not being quite as hardy as those of us who make our home this far north, most of our visitors arrive in the summer, but they're fascinated by what it's like here when it's cold. Aiming to please, Alaska's entrepreneurs have come up with not one but two ice museums, one in Fairbanks and one sixty miles northeast of Fairbanks at the Chena Hot Springs Resort (see previous entry), at the end of Chena Hot Springs Road.

The Aurora Ice Museum at Chena Hot Springs began in 2003 as an ice hotel—not the first in the world, but the first in Alaska. There you could snuggle under furs on a bed made of ice, in a room made of ice, in a structure that was part igloo and part Gothic cathedral. Fashioned of block ice with vaulting arches and an insulated exoskeleton, the hotel was cooled like a refrigerator.

It did fine in Alaska's chilly winter, but the following summer the ice hotel pulled a Frosty the Snowman and melted. Never one to give up, Chena Hot Springs owner Bernie Karl (see previous entry) hired champion ice carvers Steve and Heather Brice to reconstruct the project as an ice museum.

Oddly, the museum is kept cold with a specially designed absorption chiller powered by geothermal energy tapped from the natural hot springs on-site. Functioning on a principle similar to the effect of

60

**The ice bar at the Aurora Ice Museum at Chena Hot Springs Resort,
where your appletini served in a glass made of ice awaits**
PHOTO BY B. B. MACKENZIE

water cooling human skin as it evaporates, the energy-efficient chiller
keeps the museum intact even on Interior Alaska's warmest days,
some of which creep above ninety degrees Fahrenheit.

Visitors are invited to tour the ice museum, where colorful lights illu-
minate the Brices' sculptures. Inside the icy building, chandeliers made
of carved ice flicker like the aurora. Among the many sculptures are a
giant chess set, an ice fireplace, and life-size knights poised to joust.

There's a fairy castle feel to the place, which explains why some
choose to have their weddings inside. You can cap off your tour with

★ ★

a frosty appletini, poured at the ice bar and served in a disposable martini glass—disposable because it's made of ice, of course.

Not as impressive and only open in summer is the Fairbanks Ice Museum at 500 Second Avenue in downtown Fairbanks. A visit includes a slide show of the World Ice Art Championships (see page 83) held in Fairbanks each winter, and a big walk-in cooler where guests can see ice carvings up close.

For Those Who Can't Spell

No doubt about it: *ptarmigan* is a spelling-bee stumper. It's also Alaska's state bird. You'll find ptarmigan clucking and flapping all over the state. Not known for their brains, they are at least well-adapted for cold with their big feathered feet—the avian version of snowshoes. They also turn from brown to pure white in the winter.

So it seemed only fitting to the residents of a small gold rush town in the Interior that they name it after this adaptable if not especially brilliant bird. Trouble was, when the time came to do it, no one was sure of the spelling. So the town ended up with the name of a similarly tasty bird: Chicken.

Without its name, Chicken might have faded into oblivion as did so many other little towns that sprang up in the Fortymile mining district. But who can resist bragging about having traveled to Chicken, Alaska, population twenty or so. It's a only short jog off the Taylor Highway that runs from east of Tok and then north, connecting with the famed Top of the World Highway that leads to Dawson City on the Yukon River in Canada.

Tors

Chena River State Recreation Area

Drive northeast from Fairbanks along Chena Hot Springs Road, and you'll pass right by them without knowing they're there. But tromp off the road for a few hours and you'll come upon granite tors, several towering outcroppings of rock that rise nearly one hundred feet out of the alpine tundra.

Once a haven for miners who staked Fortymile claims, today Chicken is mostly a place to say you've been to. T-shirts, bumper stickers, coffee mugs—they sell it all. You can fill up on grub at the Chicken Creek Saloon and Cafe, the only roadhouse still standing on the Eagle Gold Rush Trail, or you can try your hand at recreational gold panning. In 1927, Chicken also became home to Anne Purdy, who immortalized her life in Chicken as a nineteen-year-old school-teacher in the popular book *Tisha.*

You may not want to stay as long as Purdy did, but you can over-night in one of Chicken's RV parks during the summer. In June you can partake of Chickenstock, a weekend music festival featuring country and bluegrass performers from around the state. Staffers in feathered helmets will direct you to a "plucking good time," be it a rendition of the crowd-pleasing "chicken dance" or chilling to your favorite tunes.

Winter is another matter: The town closes up, as does the nearby border into Canada. Best of all, thanks to the foresight of the town's founders, you won't have to sweat the spelling on those postcards to home.

★ ★

Also known as the Plain of Monuments, the tors originated as molten rock pushed up from the earth between seventy and ninety million years ago. The rock cooled before it reached the surface, and erosion has since uncovered these dramatic, jagged spires.

The fifteen-mile East Trail loop to the tors begins in the Tors Trail Campground at mile 39.5 of Chena Hot Springs Road. You'll hike through some boggy country (bring bug spray!) along the river and across Rock Creek before climbing out of the forest. A short spur trail (sometimes wet) leads to the tors, between miles five and six of the main trail. At mile nine, you'll come to another group of tors known as the Lizard's Eye. Along the way are nice views of the valley and the Alaska Range, and in the summer, you'll likely see lots of wildflowers, including anemones, poppies, and arctic harebells.

No matter where you hike in Alaska, remember that weather conditions can be unpredictable, and you need to be prepared for emergencies. Expect no amenities, bring your own food and water, and don't attempt rock climbing unless you're experienced and have the proper equipment.

Sourtoe Cocktails
Dawson City, Yukon Territory

Garnish martinis with olives and manhattans with cherries. Some even opt for tequila with worms. But at Dawson City's Downtown Hotel (1026 Second Avenue), there's only one thing to have in your drink: a real human toe.

The Sourtoe tradition began in 1973 when Capt. Dick Stevenson was telling folks about the pickled human toe he found in the cabin he'd bought. It allegedly was once attached to the foot of Louie Liken, who ran rum with his brother Otto from Canada to Alaska during Prohibition.

As the story goes, the brothers conducted their trade during blizzards so the Mounties couldn't track them. On one trip, Louie stepped in overflow—water that seeps from frozen rivers—but couldn't stop to

Take your pick: human toes to float in your Sourtoe Cocktail.
PHOTO BY B. B. MACKENZIE

care for his freezing foot because he and Otto suspected the authorities were on their tail. Sure enough, Louie's toe froze and had to be amputated. Dipping into their convenient supply of alcohol, Louie drank himself into a stupor, and Otto chopped off the toe, which they preserved in a jar of their overproof product.

Stevenson offered the toe as a novelty in a drink, and the rest is history. At first the "rules" of the Sourtoe demanded the drinker down a beer glass of Champagne until the toe touched the lips. But as people began flocking to the Downtown Hotel bar for Sourtoe Cocktails, it was decided the toe could swim in just about any old drink.

★ ★

In 1980, the growing Sourtoe tradition met with disaster: A placer miner named Gerry Younger swallowed the toe in his thirteenth drink. News outlets picked up the story, and before long a toe was donated (already amputated) to stand in. Subsequent toes have been lost and stolen, but substitutes have continued to roll in, and the bar now has a nice variety on hand so that customers can choose which to toss in their drinks. The toes are kept fresh, more or less, with alcohol and salt. Thousands have tried the Sourtoe Cocktail, which comes with a card and a certificate to prove you've accomplished the feat of downing a drink with a real human toe.

Twice Removed
Delta Junction

As gold fever swept through Alaska and the hardy stayed on, early twentieth-century roads were carved out of the wilderness. Travel wasn't easy. Horses drew stagecoaches in the summer and big sleighs in the winter, carrying passengers along primitive roads like the Valdez–Fairbanks Trail, the primary route from Interior Alaska to the ocean port of Valdez, where ships brought supplies and passage Outside.

The long and sometimes hazardous journey to Valdez was broken only by stops at roadhouses, where home-cooked meals and warm beds awaited the weary travelers.

Out of the dozens of roadhouses that served Alaska's travelers in the early decades of the 1900s, only a handful remain. One, the Historic Gakona Lodge on the Tok Cutoff fifteen miles northeast of Glenallen, was built in 1929 to replace the original roadhouse at the junction of the Valdez–Eagle and Valdez–Fairbanks Trails. You can still eat and spend the night at the Gakona Lodge, as long as you don't mind sharing space with an occasional pipe-smoking ghost.

Even more historic is the Sullivan Roadhouse, now the Sullivan Roadhouse Historical Museum. Built in 1905, the roadhouse has been moved not once but twice, log by log, earning its museum status the hard way. The Sullivan was first constructed along a winter cutoff on the then-new Valdez–Fairbanks Trail. But the cutoff proved too steep, and the Alaska Road Commission eventually shifted the trail to a flatter route some four miles away. Rather than throw in the towel, owners John and Florence Sullivan moved the roadhouse log by log to the new trail. In the process, they added a metal roof, a rarity at the time.

The metal roof spared the roadhouse from the decay its sod-roofed cousins experienced once they were abandoned, as the Sullivan was in 1923. During World War II, a military bombing range grew up along-side the old log structure, and despite nearby fires from stray ord-nance, somehow the building remained standing.

As part of an army cleanup effort, a local worker was hired to bull-doze the area around the roadhouse. But the worker couldn't bear to plow under all the artifacts he uncovered in the process, so he stashed them in his barn. The Army Legacy Fund again moved the roadhouse, log by log, using a helicopter this time. The building was reassembled in nearby Delta Junction, where, after loving restoration, it was trans-formed into a museum, creating a home for the artifacts that had been surreptitiously tucked away. The Sullivan Roadhouse Museum is now the oldest original roadhouse in Alaska's Interior.

Double-Named Mountain
Denali National Park and Preserve

Some call it Denali. Some call it McKinley. So who's got it right?

The Athabascan natives who live near the mountain have always called it Denali, meaning "the High One" or "the Great One." But newcomers to Alaska had a bad habit of ignoring traditional names, and a prospector from Ohio ended up naming the peak McKinley after William McKinley, who won his bid for the US presidency in 1896.

For years, Alaskans have tried to get the mountain's name officially changed to Denali. In 1975, the Alaska state legislature made its first approach to the US Board of Geographic Names. But it turns out that under the rules that govern the naming of United States landmarks, a name can't be changed if legislation has been introduced to block the

In a controversy almost as big as the mountain, it's offi-
cially known as McKinley, but Alaskans insist it's Denali,
Athabascan for "the High One" or the "the Great One."
Here is a sunrise view of the mountain from Wonder Lake.
PHOTO BY B. B. MACKENZIE

action. That's exactly what the Ohio congressional delegation did in
1975, and it's what they've done every year since. Unless the congress-
person from the Ohio district that includes William McKinley's hometown becomes less vigilant or concedes that it's a little strange for his
state to control the name of our mountain, it looks like our Great One
will continue to answer to two different names.

At least the official name of the park and preserve is Denali, which
is what we Alaskans also call our mountain, despite the fact that its
official name is McKinley.

★ ★

House of Rock and Ice

Denali National Park and Preserve

When it comes to building a house, everyone knows the importance of a proper foundation. But if you're determined to have the best view of North America's highest peak, you may have to make some sacrifices in that department. Famed Alaska "glacier pilot" Don Sheldon built his Mountain House in 1966 on a five-acre outcropping of rock and ice. The elevation? A whopping six thousand feet. Surrounded by glaciers, Sheldon's Mountain House is indeed one of the most scenic spots in Denali National Park.

As you might imagine, it was no small feat to build on a site this remote, with rock and ice at its foot. But Sheldon and his wife, Roberta, were no strangers to the challenges of Denali or Alaska. A legendary bush pilot, Sheldon tied building materials to the wing struts of his Cessna airplane and made multiple flights into what is now known as the Don Sheldon Ampitheater, part of the spectacular Ruth Gorge. He built the hexagonal hut with large windows, four single beds, and a woodstove.

Sheldon enjoyed his mountain house for many years before he died from cancer. Thanks to the generosity of his widow, visitors can now stay in this spectacular spot, provided they're willing to rough it a bit. It's not quite as tough as climbing North America's highest mountain, but you get a sense of what it must be like to scale through the snow and the ice, and of course there are those spectacular views. Warmed by the woodstove, you can watch hardy climbers pick their way up the mountain.

As long as you don't mind chartering a plane and hauling in your own firewood, first aid kit, water, and food, as well as hauling out the garbage and human waste, you can register with the Alaska Mountaineering Society to overnight in this most unusual of locations. Rental fees for the season (late March to mid-July) are reasonable, but this hut perched on rock and ice is so popular that it's often booked a full year ahead.

★ ★

Cheating the Mountain
Denali National Park and Preserve

Who was the first to scale Mount McKinley, the tallest North American peak? For awhile, that was a matter of some dispute. In the clamor to be first, some exaggerated claims and perhaps outright lies came to light.

First, let's admit that at 20,320 feet, North America's highest mountain isn't easy to climb. At the 60th parallel, the barometric pressure is lower than it is at other top-rated peaks, so the effect is that of climbing a 23,000 foot mountain. Weather can do a complete turnaround, often without warning. Winds exceeding one hundred miles per hour have the potential to send climbers tumbling to their deaths or flash-freeze them in wind chills that are literally off the charts.

No wonder some of the early climbers were in a big hurry to get up there, stake their claim to fame, and get back down. And without anyone to check on their progress, a wee bit of exaggeration occurred. One incident involved Dr. Frederick Cook, who in 1906 claimed his party was the first to fully ascend the mountain. But the photograph he took to substantiate his achievement turned out to be of a lower peak than the mountain's actual summit. An honest mistake? Perhaps.

Four years later, four local men attempted the summit in what was called the Sourdough Expedition. Two of them claimed to have planted a spruce pole at the mountain's north peak, but none mounted the Great One's taller south peak, and only one later climber, Hudson Stuck, was able to verify that the spruce pole had been planted. Stuck was himself the first to undisputedly reach the top of Mount McKinley in 1913, and so he is generally—and accurately—credited with the first ascent, after a few false starts by some others.

on the "slope" of
Mt. McKinley

Charlie McGonagall and Tom Lloyd of the All Alaskan
Sourdough Expedition at their fifteen-thousand-foot
level camp on Mount McKinley

Mushroom Hounds

Visit Alaska's Interior during a hot, dry summer and you're liable to get a whiff—or perhaps a choking throat full—of the smoke that comes from forest fires that burn wide swaths of land in the Interior. Come back the following summer, and you'll likely see industrious mushroom pickers scouring the charred landscape for the prize of all prizes: morels.

Those charged with managing Alaska's forests recognize that fires are part of nature's regeneration process. Old growth gives way to new, and as long as structures aren't threatened, firefighters are more likely to monitor wildfires than to try to contain them. Around places like Fairbanks, where weather patterns create natural inversions that trap wildfire smoke in the Tanana Valley, it can get pretty smoky.

The payoff comes the following year when morels repopulate the newly cleared forests. A tasty edible mushroom, the morel is easy to spot with its tall, honeycombed, spongy cap. It appears to thrive in areas of moderate burning (not too slow or too fast) that leave behind few trees but lots of organic material in the soil. Though highly sought in haute cuisine, morels are hard to grow commercially, and so a nomadic and competitive group of "shroomers" track wildfire activity so they can travel the following year in search of their fungal treasures.

If you plan to join the morel frenzy, be sure to do your homework. False morels can be deadly, and in serious burn areas, you'll likely encounter some territorial behavior among the folks who've traveled a long way in hopes the lowly mushroom will make them a fortune. If you're picking for your own fun and eating pleasure, keep in mind that morels that have been on the stalk for too long can get wormy; soaking in lemon juice and water is said to flush out the worms. Remember, too, that it takes a whopping ten to fifteen pounds of fresh morels to get one pound of dehydrated mushrooms.

Locked for All Time
Denali National Park and Preserve

A sure sign of autumn in Alaska is when moose are in rut. It's the time of year you're most likely to see, and to hear, big bull moose asserting their claims for the cows. Bulls will charge one another, grunting and huffing, their antlers clattering as they crash together.

The remains of two battling bulls, antlers locked for all time
PHOTO BY B. B. MACKENZIE

★ ★

Sometimes the battle turns deadly. That's what happened back in 2003 near Moose Creek in Denali National Park and Preserve, when two bull moose locked antlers. The eye of one of the bulls was pierced through, and both animals died. You can see the legacy of these two determined creatures at the new Eielson Visitor Center at mile 66 of the Denali Park Road.

Jurassic Alaska
Denali National Park and Preserve

No snakes, no lizards, no lumbering tortoises. Cold-blooded reptiles can't survive in Alaska. But millions of years ago, dinosaurs roamed freely here. In fact, our Denali National Park is home to more diverse dinosaur fossils than any other national park, with the exception of Dinosaur Monument.

Evidence that thunder lizards had free rein in the north surfaced in a 1975 with a photograph of a three-toed track taken in a remote part of Alaska near the Bering Sea. But without data to pinpoint the location, thirty-five years passed before scientists were able to revisit the site. In the meantime, the fossilized track of a theropod, a meat eater, was found near Igloo Creek in Denali Park, setting off a series of expeditions that unearthed evidence of plant-eating hadrosaurs along with other plant and animal life from the Cretaceous period, some seventy million years ago.

Fossil sites along Denali's Cantwell Formation now number in the hundreds. Students, interns, and volunteers turn out every summer to help scientists comb several stratigraphic layers. Their finds include fossils of dinosaur feces and skin as well as the remains of small mammals, plants, and fish. In time, researchers hope to piece together a full Cretaceous ecosystem.

But to return to that lingering question of the three-toed print photographed in 1975: A team of geologists and paleontologists returned to the Chignik Bay area to investigate, and amazingly it took only two days for them to locate the tracks, which are at such a vertical angle

★ ★

that they can only be reached with climbing equipment. The fossilized evidence, which includes the tips of the dinosaur's claws, indicates that a human-sized, meat-eating theropod strolled on what was once a sandy beach a whopping fifty million years before dinosaurs tromped through Denali.

Denali Road Lottery
Denali National Park and Preserve

It's no Powerball, and the prize is a lot more elusive than cash. Yet Alaskans enter in droves every year, taking their chances in one of the state's most popular lotteries, the Denali Road Lottery. The prize: a pass that lets them drive the full 184 miles of the Denali Park Road in their own private vehicle, at their own pace, stopping wherever they choose, along with 399 other lucky winners.

A grizzly bear sow and two cubs along Denali Park Road
PHOTO BY B. B. MACKENZIE

★ ★

When the George Parks Highway opened in 1972, the Denali Park Road was closed to private vehicle traffic. Unless you have a media or concessionaire permit, your only access beyond the park's entrance area is on one of the sanctioned, scheduled buses. At first, park officials allowed private vehicles in for a few weeks in September, after the shuttle system closed down for the season. But in 1989, over 1,500 vehicles clogged the road in one day, a fiasco that resulted in the current lottery system.

Road lottery hopefuls must enter in June with a ten dollar application fee. They can designate their preference of three of the four days that the road will be open. Based on previous years' interest, the odds of winning one of the lucrative park road passes are actually pretty decent—about one in six.

What you'll see on your drive through the park is anyone's guess. Some years wolf packs with their growing pups are spotted near the road. Some years real-time drama unfolds, with wolves tracking and

Fata Morgana

What force can smash mountains? Fata Morgana may not truly squash our big mountains, but it creates that illusion.

The complex mirage known as Fata Morgana is named for Morgan le Fay, the legendary sister of King Arthur who learned magic from Merlin. It only occurs during weather inversions, when cold air is trapped near the ground under a layer of warm air. The inversion causes light to bend toward the cold as the images superimpose one over the other. As the layers shift, the image appears to reshape, so that large objects like mountains look boxy or smashed.

taking a caribou. Moose go in rut that time of year, so there's a good chance of spotting an amorous bull in pursuit of a cow. But most of the prize involves the freedom to travel the road at your own pace, without the hoards of tourists that pile on the buses each day during the regular season.

Dropped in Their Tracks
Dyea

Boots. Pots. Pans. Stoves. Tin cans. Wrenches. Cables. What's a miner to do when the load is too heavy to haul? Start dumping.

That's what prospectors did as they climbed through the Chilkoot Pass, where historical artifacts from the Klondike gold rush still litter the trail right where they were dropped. Hike the trail and you'll discover all sorts of rusty remnants bearing witness to the toll this route took on the miners.

In July of 1897, ships pulled into ports in San Francisco and Seattle bearing a ton of gold extracted from the Klondike district, deep in the heart of Canada's Yukon Territory. With the US economy in a recession, there was even more than the usual interest in making a quick fortune, and the rush was on. Steamship companies, standing to profit from the traffic, painted a rosy picture of the prospects. Tens of thousands streamed north, most with little idea of how tough it was to actually get to the Klondike.

Those with ample money could afford the long but relatively easy water route, sailing by steamer from Seattle to the Bering Sea, then up the Yukon River, across Alaska, and into Dawson City, Canada, near Bonanza Creek, where the first big strike was made. The river route took lots of time, but provisions could be neatly tucked away in the hull of the boat, and for the most part the prospectors arrived with their belongings intact. There was also an all-Canadian overland route, but it was rugged and long, so few ventured that way.

The rest ended up on the Chilkoot, a virtual pedestrian highway that replaced the ill-fated White Horse route through the mountains

One of many shoes left behind on the famed Chilkoot Trail
PHOTO BY B. B. MACKENZIE

from Skagway, where horses faltered and fell from the steep, muddy excuse for a trail. In contrast, the Chilkoot, which began in Dyea, was a fairly direct route over the mountains. Used by coastal Indians to trade with tribes in the Interior, the Chilkoot was proven, but not easy. Called "the meanest thirty-three miles in history," much of it angles at forty-five degrees through the mountains.

The first wave of prospectors to hit Dawson City was poorly provisioned, and a famine resulted during the winter of 1897. To prevent a recurrence, Canadian authorities began requiring stampeders to bring one ton of supplies on their trek. On the Chilkoot, these goods had to be trudged up the mountain on the backs of the men (and a few women). Thirty to forty trips hauling fifty- to sixty-pound loads were required.

* *

Walk the trail today—it's still a mean thirty-three miles—and you'll understand why some of them had second thoughts about what they might need. Miners shed anything from their loads that wasn't essential—shoes, tools, pots, pans, even stoves and washing machines.

A half mile from the summit, at a point called the Scales where hired packers weighed their loads and often upped the charge for their services, the piles of stuff left behind grow even larger. Even those packing their own goods dumped gear before they reached the famed "golden stairs"—the steepest section of trail. Strewn with the rubble are parts of trams erected in 1900 to lighten the loads of the miners—but by 1900, the rush was all but over.

Among the most curious artifacts are dozens of canvas boats left to rot at a point not far from the summit. Boats were needed because on the other side of the mountains, starting at Lake Bennett, the prospectors had to navigate five hundred miles of river to reach Dawson City. Not everyone had the skills to build their own boats, and the canvas boats were evidently meant to provide a tidy solution—and a tidy profit for the businessmen who concocted the plan. But someone forgot to take note that Lake Bennett is on the Canadian side, and with no money for tariffs, they abandoned the project at the top of the mountain, adding another exhibit to what amounts to a big outdoor museum, the Chilkoot Trail in the Klondike Gold Rush National Historical Park.

Self-Dentistry, Alaska Style
Eagle

Some unusual characters have made Alaska their home, and among the most unusual ranks Nimrod Robertson, the miner from Eagle who made his own set of dentures out of a melted aluminum lid, bear molars, caribou premolars, and Dall sheep incisors.

The 1898 Klondike gold rush brought Robertson (born Edwin) from Maine to Alaska, where he settled in the Yukon River town of Eagle, established by miners disgruntled that all the Canadian claims had

★ ★

been taken. The town's founders staked out two hundred lots, offering each for a five dollar recording fee and a promise to build. Within a year, two hundred cabins had sprung up in Eagle, mostly rough little places with sod roofs.

It was in such a cabin that Nimrod Robertson, known for his ingenuity, got laid up with a horrible toothache. It's said that he yanked out every last tooth with a pair of pliers, then set to work fashioning their replacements from animal teeth. Next to Nimrod, George Washington with his wooden dentures seems rather ho-hum.

And the old timer's claim to fame doesn't stop there. Rumor has it that despite his own set of borrowed teeth, he was terrified of being eaten by wild animals. When he got lost in a blinding blizzard, he pulled up his parka hood, folded his arms over his chest, crossed his legs, and lay down in a fast moving stream, where he froze in a chunk of ice that shielded him from scavengers.

Strange, yes. True? Probably. You can see Nimrod's fancy teeth for yourself at the Eagle Historical Society and Museum at the corner of First and Berry Streets (907-547-2325).

Skinny Dick's Halfway Inn
Ester

Halfway between Fairbanks and Nenana, this popular watering hole at mile 328 of the Parks Highway is not exactly family fare, but it's a fun stop for adults. If you miss the first clue—the name—there's also their trademark logo featuring a couple of polar bears busy doing what polar bears do—making baby bears.

In case the general free-for-all atmosphere that's made Skinny's an Alaskan icon doesn't come across through either the name or the visual aid, there's also a sign outside warning patrons to expect "adult humor." The sign goes on in some detail about what that includes, so if you're traveling with children, you'd best avoid the sign, too.

The adult humor extends to the gift shop, where items for sale include not only T-shirts and baseball caps with Skinny's trademark

★ ★

Skinny Dick's Halfway Inn makes the most of its name.
PHOTO BY G. M. FERENCY

Halfway Inn logo, but also ladies' lingerie and unique women's halter tops made from men's underwear. If you want to prove you've brushed up against Alaska's underbelly on your trip north, you don't dare go home without a Skinny Dick's souvenir.

As for Skinny himself, it's said he landed in the North Country in the early 1970s. The rustic living suited him fine, and he had no qualms about running a bar without electricity. They don't make bars like that anymore, and they don't make bartenders like Skinny either. As for the bears, our research indicates that theirs is a timeless pursuit.

Flour from Ice

Alaska's rivers and streams run in some unusual colors: gray, blue-green, even milky white. This coloring is a sure sign that the water is thick with glacial "flour," or silt. While the old saying that glacial rivers are too thick to plow and too dry to drink is a bit of an exaggeration, it's true that the silt carried by glacial melt is curious stuff.

One of the best places to see how glacial silt colors water is at the confluence of a glacial and a nonglacial river. A ride on the riverboat *Discovery* in Fairbanks will take you to the place where the Chena, a typical Interior waterway brown with tannins, meets the Tanana, which comes out of a glacier. At their junction, the brown swirls into gray, a clear visual for the two types of water.

A hiker crosses a dry channel of glacial silt.
PHOTO BY G. M. FERENCY

A more technical term for glacial flour or silt is *drift,* a word that refers to any sediment, large or small, scraped from the land by a glacier. Flour is the smallest of these particles, nearly microscopic, and though in glacial areas it covers the ground like dirt, it's more powdery, silken, and white-gray than dirt. Suspended in water, it's amazingly heavy; many a good swimmer has unfortunately drowned in Alaska's rivers, weighed down by the silt that gets in their clothes.

Wind-blown silt, known as loess, also accounts for some of the remarkable fossils preserved in Alaska. Much of the Alaska rock from which glacial flour is ground is calcareous, which means it is able to neutralize acids that would otherwise eat away at skeletal remains. Thanks to this flour, bones some fifty thousand years old still contain marrow and other organic material that allow scientists to examine their ancient DNA structures.

Short-Lived Art

Fairbanks

In Fairbanks each February, master ice sculptors come from all over the world to carve intricate, towering creations. But a few weeks later, when the March sun hints of spring, their masterpieces begin to melt.

Since 1995, Fairbanks has hosted the World Ice Art Championships. Over a hundred artists compete in single- and multi-block events, carving big blocks of ice with chisels and chain saws. At first, ice for the event was hauled up from Seattle, until someone realized—duh—Fairbanks has plenty of ice. And as it turns out, ice harvested from the local O'Grady Pond is so exceptionally clear that it's now called "Arctic Diamond." Harvesting ice for the event—over 1,500 tons of it—requires forklifts, very long chain saws, and dedicated volunteers. To aid in the process, one long-term volunteer even designed a special jig for the saw to make cutting less strenuous.

In the single-block competition, one or two carvers work ice that's 5 by 8 by 3 feet—a whopping 7,800-pound chunk. Working around the clock, competitors have sixty hours to shape their projects, which are judged at night under white lights. In the multi-block competition, teams of two to four sculptors work ten blocks of ice, each measuring 4 by 6 by 3.3 feet. That's 46,000 pounds of ice for each sculpture, with some finished products towering over twenty feet tall. Unlike the single-block competition, in this division the sculptors are allowed to move their blocks with the help of heavy equipment.

Along with the fine art on display at the Ice Park, there's also fun for the younger set at the Kids Park, including ice mazes, ice slides, and ice sculptures to play on. Ice Alaska, host of the World Ice Art Championships, also offers classes for carvers both young and old. Young artists learn design and engraving skills that transfer to ice carving, while adults learn to use chain saws, die grinders, blowtorches, and chisels to shape ice into their masterpieces.

Part of the novelty, of course, is that ice doesn't last forever, even in the subarctic. By mid-March, the spring weather has typically taken

So Far Away and Yet So Close Together, 2010 NICA Qualifier
competition at the BP World Ice Art Championships, created
by James Stugart over twenty-four hours within two days
PHOTO BY JAMES STUGART

its toll on the sculptures. The sun burns the ice, making it brittle and
opaque, and warm winds polish and erode its surface as the warm
temperatures cause a meltdown. For best viewing, plan a visit shortly
after the judging in early March, and be sure to visit the Ice Park at
night, when colored lights make it seem like a fairyland made of ice.
To get details on dates and locations, go to www.icealaska.com.

Roadster Relics
Fairbanks

Our state has few roads and not many antiques, so an antique car museum is one of the last things you'd expect to find here. Yet one has sprung up in Fairbanks—a good one—on a hotel property belonging to Fountainhead, one of the largest hotel and property management companies in Alaska.

The Fountainhead Antique Auto Museum is the farthest north car museum in the country. It features over seventy classic cars, several of which are the only ones left of their type, like the 1920 Argonne and

**Antique cars and vintage clothing on display at the
Fountainhead Antique Auto Museum**
PHOTO BY KAELA TANNER

the 1898 Hay Motor Carriage. Most of the rare cars are restored to working condition, though a few remain as they were found.

Large photos documenting the history of motor travel in Alaska line the walls of the museum. Along with archival movie footage, they document the ingenuity of Alaskans in adapting their vehicles to our unique conditions, with modifications resulting in cars that cut firewood, rode over railroad tracks, and traveled on snow.

For those who tire of engines and chassis, there are displays of fifty types of vintage clothing connected with the automobile. You can even dress up in old-style clothes and get your photo taken with your own camera behind the wheel of one of the cars in the Valdez–Fairbanks Trail display.

Even non-motorheads will be won over by the story of young Bobby Sheldon, who in 1905 built Alaska's very first car from the wheels up, all in hopes of winning the affections of a certain young lady. After studying magazine photos, Sheldon assembled the car using barroom chairs, buggy wheels, and a two-cycle marine engine. Reportedly, Sheldon's vehicle clocked out at a whopping fifteen miles per hour.

The Fountainhead Antique Auto Museum is on the grounds of the Wedgewood Resort at 212 Wedgewood Drive (907-450-2100).

Midnight Sun Baseball
Fairbanks

It's been going on for over a hundred years: baseball at midnight, with no artificial lights, as a unique way to celebrate the summer solstice in Interior Alaska.

A booming little town that served as a supply center for gold camps throughout the Tanana River Valley, Fairbanks was only five years old when the first midnight sun pitch was tossed in 1906. Looking down from what's now called Pedro Dome, one of the hills that hem in the valley, Felix Pedro envisioned the potential at the confluence of the Chena and Tanana Rivers, but he likely never suspected the fad that midnight sun baseball would become.

★ ★

**An archival photograph depicts the annual
midnight baseball game; the caption
says the photo was taken at midnight.**
UAF-1989-166-553, ARCHIVES, UNIVERSITY OF ALASKA FAIRBANKS

The Goldpanners, Fairbanks's minor league team, play all summer
long. Talented sluggers travel from the Lower 48 to live with host
families in the land of the midnight sun, honing skills that often propel
them into major league play. Dozens and sometimes hundreds of spectators turn out to watch them each summer, but during the solstice
game each June 21, the stands at Growden Memorial Park at the corner of Second Avenue and Wilbur Street are packed with fans. It's not
every day you get to watch live baseball at midnight.

The park seats approximately 3,500, though reportedly some 5,200
packed in for the Midnight Sun Game in 1967, when a Japanese team
played the Goldpanners. Growden Park does have artificial lights for
gloomy nights late in the season, but light from the sun is plenty for
most games.

★ ★

Because the angled light at the top of the world can be almost blinding, smart players and fans don sunglasses, even at midnight. Technically, the sun does set in Fairbanks—it's 188 miles south of the Arctic Circle—but on June 21 what counts as night is a wee bit of twilight as the sun dips ever so slightly below the horizon and pops up again.

Colorful Joe
Fairbanks

Alaska has its share—maybe more than its share—of colorful figures, independent and larger than life. One of the most colorful was Joe Vogler, the well-known contrarian who founded the Alaska Independence Party and advocated for Alaska's secession from the Union.

Often seen sporting a gray fedora, Vogler was never shy about expressing his opinions. After earning a law degree from the University of Kansas, Vogler moved to Kodiak in 1942 and a year later to Fairbanks, where he worked for the US Army Corps of Engineers and took up mining. He acquired hundreds of acres of what is now prime real estate north of Fairbanks off the Steese Highway and Farmers Loop Road. When he later subdivided and sold off the land, he insisted on covenants banning the area's ubiquitous cottonwood trees from the new developments.

Vogler's reputation as a rabble-rouser extended far beyond landscaping. He documented numerous complaints in letters to the editor of the *Fairbanks Daily News-Miner.* He filed suit in 1948 against a bus company for using a bridge that was too narrow for the bus to stay on its side of the center line. In 1973, he circulated a petition calling for Alaska's secession from the United States. He organized the Alaskans for Independence to actively pursue secession while he continued work with the Alaskan Independence Party to question the legitimacy of the 1958 Statehood Act. Claiming an intense hatred for the federal government, he insisted that he would never be buried on American soil.

★ ★

Vogler made several unsuccessful runs for Alaska governor, gaining even more notoriety for reportedly advocating that the state "nuke the glaciers" in order to build a highway to Juneau.

In May of 1993, Vogler disappeared. His remains were discovered nearly eighteen months later at a gravel pit outside of town, presumably dumped by Manfried West, who was convicted of murdering Vogler over a transaction involving plastic explosives.

From within the Alaska Independence Party, there is still discussion about whether Vogler's murder stemmed from a larger plot to silence him before he could testify before the United Nations concerning his assertion that the Alaska Statehood Act violated a UN charter signed by the United States. True to his wishes, Vogler was buried in Dawson City, Yukon Territory.

Rock, Skip, Score
Fairbanks

What sorts of entertainment get Alaskans through our long, cold winters? Aside from the historic, tried-and-true saloon-related pastimes— or rather capitalizing on the bar interest—there's curling.

Scottish immigrants eager for Klondike gold brought the sport to Dawson City in 1898. A few years later, the rush moved to Fairbanks, and curling went with it. In 1905, the oldest of all sporting clubs in Alaska was formed: the Fairbanks Curling Club.

For the first couple of seasons, hardy curlers tossed their rocks outside on the Chena River and along the Northern Commercial Company dock. In 1908, Alaska's first curling club, with two sheets of ice, was built in downtown Fairbanks. Socializing, a large component of curling, had to be done in warmer buildings. Eventually the club expanded to sheets in an indoor facility that hosts several bonspiels each season, including one for the curling hardy that runs all night and all day. Though Fairbanks hosts the largest club in Alaska, there's also a club in Anchorage, and it's rumored some curling—not for the meek—goes on outdoors in Barrow.

★ ★

Curling on indoor rinks offers lively competition during Alaska's long winters.
PHOTO BY G. M. FERENCY

Curling has grown from a curious beer-drinking pastime to a serious Olympic event. Even in Alaska, the rocks, polished granite with handles, are imported from a single quarry in Scotland. Though the rock is said to be thrown, modern curlers actually slide the rock on the ice, propelling it mostly with the thrust of one leg off a wedge in the ice called the hack. The rock is let go with a twist, causing it to spin and curve, or curl, as it speeds down the ice toward the spot indicated by the skip, the team captain who plots and directs each throw. Sweepers work the ice in front of the rocks, creating friction that melts a thin film on the ice to straighten the rock's trajectory, speeding it toward the concentric circles of the house, where points are scored with a system that's nearly as curious as the sport itself.

★ ★

Even in the rough and rowdy gold rush days, curling maintained its reputation as a gentleperson's game. Matches begin with handshakes all around and end with the affirmation "Good Curling" proclaimed by both winners and losers. And good form continues with friendly rounds of drinks at the bar, a curling-club fixture.

Northern Bats

Most of our visitors come north with the idea of spotting some sort of wildlife: bear, moose, caribou, wolves, fox, and the like. Some fix their eyes on the skies, knowing the arctic and subarctic are among the most prime nesting grounds for migratory birds. What you're unlikely to find are folks explicitly seeking those mammals that remind us of birds: bats.

You might think that bats are too thin-skinned and lightly furred to live this far north. While it's true they don't hang around in the winter, migratory bats hang out in the Yukon Territory and Interior Alaska during the summer months. Both megabats—the big guys—and microbats are found here. No one knows why they don't range much higher than the 64 degrees north latitude, but it may have something to do with the fact that colder nights to the north cut down on the nocturnal insects on which bats feed.

Venturing farther north would also take bats too far from their hibernation sites. Bat hibernation caves have been confirmed on Prince of Wales Island in Southeast Alaska, and there are suspected hibernation sites in other parts of the region. During hibernation, a bat's heart rate drops from between one hundred and two hundred beats per minute at rest to just twenty. They can also stop breathing for up to forty-eight minutes.

★ ★

Alaska's Big Burps
Fairbanks

There's no polite way to say it. Alaska's lakes are, well, burping. Specifically, some of them burp methane, a gas that's twenty-five times more potent in its greenhouse effects than carbon dioxide.

Here's what happens: As permafrost around Alaska's lakes melts, organic material that had been trapped in the frozen soils drops to the bottom of nearby lakes. There it decomposes, releasing methane gas. In the summer, the methane burped by Alaska's lakes bubbles into the air without much notice. Come winter, the gas concentrates in opaque bubbles trapped in the lake ice—frozen burps, if you will.

Pop a methane bubble with a big ice pick, light a match, and you've got methane-burp pyrotechnics. University of Alaska assistant professor Katey Walter Anthony and her scientific team have filmed some dramatic footage documenting the explosive nature of these big Alaskan burps.

Beyond the dramatic flares when methane ignites, how exactly does one study methane produced by melting permafrost? One method, believe it or not, is to collect the gas in plastic garbage bags for transport back to the lab. That's one of the ways Anthony and her team conduct ongoing research on the impact of melting permafrost on the earth's changing climate.

Where trees lean and ground cover collapses, there's generally melting permafrost, and you won't have to look far for a burping lake. Anthony predicts that if current trends continue, Alaska's lakes will burp ten times the methane that's currently in the atmosphere. So the problem amounts to a lot more than table manners, which is why she and her fellow scientists continue their studies.

Pope Meets Saloon

Fairbanks

What do you do when the pope's visit is over and you're not sure what to do with the nice red carpet you laid down for him to walk over? In Fairbanks, the papal red carpet landed in a most unlikely place: onstage at one of the state's best-known saloons.

The fact that a pope even came through Alaska is a curiosity all on its own. Pope John Paul II made only seven visits to the United States during his papacy, and two of these, oddly enough, were stopovers in Alaska on his way somewhere else: one in Anchorage in 1981, and one in Fairbanks in 1984. The stop in Fairbanks on May 2, 1984, was especially historic, because the pope's layover coincided with President Reagan's stopover there, and so the two went tête-à-tête. The town of Fairbanks, often considered a stepchild to Anchorage, hosted the first-ever meeting of a pope with a US president outside the White House or the Vatican.

Naturally, there was a bit of hoopla to go along with such a momentous occasion. The room where the two dignitaries met at the Fairbanks airport, dubbed the Pope-President Room, is marked with a plaque.

But since Fairbanks doesn't get a whole lot of celebrities passing through, there was no further use for the red carpet. So Fairbanks attorney Bill Satterberg and Howling Dog Saloon owner Mike Brock each ponied up to purchase half of the six-foot by ninety-eight-foot rug. It was installed on the saloon's stage in 1985, where countless rock-and-roll musicians have now foot stomped where the pope once trod.

The Howling Dog, also known as "the bar where the dawgs howl and the kittens drink free," is a sometimes boisterous, eclectic party stop in Fox, a small community ten miles north of Fairbanks. Located on the Old Steese Highway near the Turtle Club and the Silver Gulch

Brewery (see page 114), the Dog is known mostly for its fun-loving crowds and its lively atmosphere, but if you happen to get up on stage, there's that carpet, still rocking after all these years.

Ice Fog
Fairbanks

When temperatures creep to thirty degrees below zero Fahrenheit and colder during long Fairbanks winters, residents brace for an inevitable and unwelcome visitor: ice fog.

Ice fog forms because in extreme cold, the air quickly saturates, unable to hold the water that is a normal part of what we breathe. Tiny droplets of water unleashed by car engines, power plants, humans, and even dogs instantly turn to even tinier droplets of ice that hang in the air, sometimes for days and even weeks.

Though ice fog can occur anyplace where extreme cold lasts for more than a day or two, it's especially bad in Fairbanks, where the surrounding hills create a temperature inversion that traps the cold near ground. Drive from town to the hills during one of these cold snaps, and you'll burst from the oppressive gray fog into sunlight.

The fog was especially bad during the mid-1970s when the oil pipeline boom was in full swing. Lots of people, lots of cars, lots of people who didn't shut off their cars—afraid their cars wouldn't start again, some left them running nonstop for the whole winter. Back then, too, there weren't engine heaters so that cars could be plugged in, a practice that not only helps cars start in the cold but also one that reduces the emissions that contribute to ice fog.

Has Anyone Seen My Northern Lights?
Fairbanks

What's green and red and purple all over? That would be Alaska's night sky when the aurora borealis, or northern lights, are active. Mysterious and evocative, these lights swirl with as much fantasy as fact.

★ ★

According to some legends, whistling summons the northern lights. According to others, whistling chases them off. Some fear that the displays call on the spirits of the dead or that they broadcast omens portending disaster. Rumor has it that some Japanese tourists believe that children conceived under the northern lights will be especially bright.

Because the massive lights bend over the curved surface of the earth, they give the illusion of touching the ground when in fact they dip only as close as sixty miles from the surface. Though some report hearing a crackling with especially vivid displays, the noise-making capability of the aurora has never been proven.

What causes this mysterious nighttime phenomenon? Though the sun is scarce on Alaska's short winter days, it makes itself known during our nights, when solar winds kick up charged particles that blast toward earth at speeds topping one million miles per hour. Drawn to the earth's magnetic poles, these wind-borne electrons collide with oxygen to make green and with nitrogen to make pinkish red, purple, and blue.

While the ground temperature has nothing to do with whether the aurora will be active, it is true that the lights are easiest to see on the clear, dark nights of a high-pressure cold spells. For the best viewing, you'll want to get far from the lights of even our small cities. That's what the aurora photographers do, suffering many a long and cold winter night in hopes of catching a glimpse of this unique phenomenon.

Maybe because they start coming out about the time our last summer guests say goodbye, Alaskans feel as entitled to the northern lights as they do to the Permanent Fund Dividend checks that distribute a share of the earnings from Alaska's oil. Newspapers forecast the lights much as they do the weather. But that could all change. The earth's magnetic poles are constantly changing, and if the North Pole continues moving as it has for the past century or so, it could end up in Siberia within a few decades, robbing Alaska of most of its auroral activity.

★ ★

Lucky Thirteen
Fairbanks

It's tough to explain this kind of luck, unless you're Lance Mackey. He credits lucky bib number thirteen, the same bib his brother and father wore in their respective Iditarod wins, with his sweep of not one but two long-distance sled-dog races in 2006. He's gone on to win several more, earning recognition as one of Alaska's most successful long-distance mushers.

To get bib thirteen, Mackey camped seven nights in front of the Iditarod headquarters in Wasilla. He was no stranger to camping, having pitched a tent for the summer with his new wife and her daughters on a Kenai Peninsula beach when they began their new life together. He was no stranger to luck, either, but to that point it had been mostly the hard kind. He'd grown up in a dog-mushing family, but his adult life got off to a rocky start, and after his first comeback Iditarod run in 2001, he discovered the pain plaguing his jaw was not an abscessed tooth but cancer.

Determination has a way of turning luck on its ear, and Mackey proved he had plenty of that. His dogs played no small part in his turn-around. A few minutes spent watching Mackey interact with his team will confirm their devotion to him, and his devotion to them. In 2007, on a last-minute whim, Mackey took most of the dogs he was saving for the high-stakes, thousand-plus-mile Iditarod Sled Dog Race and signed on for the less-famed but grueling Yukon Quest. On the trail between Whitehorse, Yukon Territory, and Fairbanks, the more Mackey's dogs ran, the faster they went, bringing home a first-place trophy. Then Mackey did the unthinkable, mushing all but three of those same dogs to Nome a month later, finishing again in first place.

Among Mackey's competitors, theories ran wild about how dogs broken in on the Quest might be better able to metabolize fat, while teams better rested require a few days on the trail before they make the same shift. There has also been some understandable envy as

Lance Mackey, one of the winningest mushers in Iditarod race history, at the start of the 2010 race
PHOTO BY G. M. FERENCY

Mackey took the Iditarod win, with its huge cash purse and new truck, again in 2007, 2008, 2009, and 2010. There was even some bickering over Mackey's prescription for medical marijuana, resulting in drug tests for mushers in the 2010 race—tests Mackey passed along with the others.

Mackey takes the reactions in stride with his typical grin. For his strong string of wins, he credits his dogs and their spirit—and a little luck from lucky bib number thirteen.

★ ★

Farming for Fur
Fairbanks

Farming in Alaska has never been easy, but during the early days of the territory, it was difficult to get fresh meats and produce without some attempt at agriculture. Cattle were ranched on Kodiak Island, and reindeer were herded on the Seward Peninsula near Nome.

Art with Some Hair on It

"Art with some hair on it"—that's how Fairbanks artist Sandy Jamieson describes his colorful paintings that evoke amusement and admiration.

In Jamieson's paintings, Alaska's large mammals—bears, moose, caribou, wolves—swap places with humans. In *Alaska Frisbee*, a wolf leaps to grab a small plane in its teeth. The *More-Oil Majority* features a bear driving a motorcycle along the Trans Alaska oil pipeline with a copy of Sandy's Permanent Fund Dividend check (reflecting a citizen's share of the state's oil proceeds) plastered on the front of his ride. *Wildlife Refuge* depicts the Senator's Saloon at the Pump House Restaurant in Fairbanks, 796 Chena Pump Road, populated with wild animals enjoying libations. In *Local Hire*, beavers and bears join firefighters to save a historic building near the Clay Street Cemetery in Fairbanks.

His summer gig as a bush pilot and guide no doubt informs his winter work at the easel. To see Sandy's paintings and prints, visit the Aurora Gallery at 737 West Fifth Avenue in Anchorage, or go to Jamieson's website at www.sandyjamieson.com.

★ ★

In addition, vegetables and dairy products were cultivated in the Interior and Southcentral Alaska, where long summer days presented an opportunity for fast-growing plants that thrived in cool soils. In fact, the first college in the Interior was a school of agriculture and mining, now the University of Alaska Fairbanks.

A polar bear stacks the deck in Jamieson's *A Tip from Santa.*
PHOTO BY B. B. MACKENZIE

★ ★

In this archival photo, a maternally inclined cat at the Alaska Silver Fox and Fur Company in Fairbanks tends to fox kits.
LIBRARY OF CONGRESS, MRS. W. CHAPIN HUNTINGTON, 1915

For a short while during the 1920s, farming of a different sort took hold in the Interior: fox farming. It was an enterprise begun by the Russians, who established fox farms in the Aleutian Islands as early as the eighteenth century. After World War I, an increased worldwide demand for fur led Fairbanks entrepreneurs to start farming fox. The market crashed during the Depression, and Alaska's fox farms disappeared.

★ ★

Blue Babe

Fairbanks

Paul Bunyan's blue ox Babe is the stuff of legend, but Alaska's Blue Babe is the real thing, a steppe bison preserved in permafrost since the Ice Age.

A gold-mining family discovered Blue Babe near Fairbanks in 1952 while using a hydraulic hose to melt frozen soils. As if uncovering an Ice Age relic weren't unusual enough, the exposed portions of the carcass turned blue when exposed to air, the result of a reaction between

**The remains of Blue Babe, the Ice Age bison on display
at the University of Alaska Museum of the North**
PHOTO BY KAELA TANNER

the phosphorus in the mammal's tissues and the iron in the surrounding soils.

Under the direction of a team of scientists from the University of Alaska, the bison was extracted with great care. Surrounding soils were gathered and sifted as part of the study. Carbon dating places the bison's age at thirty-six thousand years.

The soils had preserved the bison so well that it told the story of its own death. Claw marks and bite wounds indicate it was attacked by an Ice Age American lion, a distant relative of today's African lion. It appears to have been killed during the winter, when freezing kept the carcass from being completely scavenged. Though the bison's hair is mostly decomposed, its hooves are intact, as are the horn sheaths. Blue Babe was reconstructed by a taxidermist and is now one of the favorite curiosities on display at the University of Alaska Museum of the North.

Because of its discontinuous permafrost, the Fairbanks area is a treasure trove for Ice Age creatures. In addition to Blue Babe, a partial baby mammoth carcass was uncovered there and transported to the American Museum of Natural History in New York, where it is maintained in a refrigerated display. And a few years back, an elementary school student walking home from school on the west side of Fairbanks stumbled on an intact woolly mammoth tusk.

Fire from Ice
Fairbanks

Start with a sheet of smooth, clear ice, the kind you find only in places like Fairbanks, where crystalline blocks cut from local lakes are used in the annual World Ice Art Championship (see page 83), a spectacular event attracting over one hundred competitors and forty-four thousand visitors.

Once you've found your perfect ice, you'll need to shave down the ends so it bulges in the middle like a magnifying glass. Then you wait for a sunny, clear day. Never mind that it's cold. Very cold.

In 2007, Ross Hanson and his ice-carving team followed this recipe to prove that you can make fire from ice. After carving for days, they produced a three-foot ice lens, positioning it so it gathered enough midwinter rays to light a piece of newsprint on fire.

Fire or ice? We'll take both, thank you.

Sun Dogs

All over Alaska, but especially in the frosty Interior, a common midwinter sight is frosty rainbows on either side of the sun. A similar effect creates multicolored halos around the moon or the sun, as well as vertical pillars of light extending from street lights.

The effect is caused by ice crystals that reflect and refract light. The optical effect on street lights is white, caused purely by reflection. But sun dogs—the rainbows on either side of the sun—are rainbow colored because the light is refracted by the ice crystals. Sun dogs are especially prevalent in places where the sun hangs low in the sky, as it does for most of Alaska's winter.

★ ★

Fort Knox Alaska
Fairbanks

If you're sad to have missed out on Alaska's multiple rushes for gold, you'll be pleased to know a bit of wild chase continues. As gold prices soar, new technology helps miners get gold from where they couldn't before. One result: Alaska's Fort Knox.

Bunny Boots

It's no small trick, keeping those tootsies warm at forty below. When it's that cold, only one type of footwear will do: the bunny boot.

There's nothing fuzzy or furry about this rabbit's foot. In fact, these unwieldy boots are more reminiscent of Bigfoot than of the Easter bunny. They're heavy and ugly but warm: three layers of one-quarter-inch wool, a one-inch felt sole, and a valve for releasing pressure from the boot in case you happen to find yourself trapped in an unpressurized aircraft or attempting the summit of one of Alaska's big mountains. The valve gave rise to the myth that the boots are inflated with air, when in fact it's the layers of felt sealed within two layers of rubber that keep insulation from soaking up sweat, which is a main cause of cold. Between with sealed rubber keeping things dry and the big soles that keep your feet off the ground, you'll have to find some other cause for complaint than cold feet.

Bunny boots come in two fashion shades: black and white. Though the white boots get scuffed and dirty, they're designed to withstand more cold than the black ones, and so it's the white you'll likely see tromping the woods—and sometimes the streets—of our state. It's also the white that earned these boots their name, after the

At Fort Knox in Kentucky, the US government stores its reserves of gold—a whopping 147 million ounces of it. That's a wee bit more than Alaska's Fort Knox, but then miners, like anglers, have been known to overstate things a bit.

Out of season, bunny boots nestle on a fine Alaska lawn.
PHOTO BY G. M. FERENCY

snowshoe hare, which does pretty well in the winter with its big white feet.

You won't find bunny boots at any of those fancy upscale shoe stores. Originally military issue, the real things come from army surplus stores. In Anchorage, try the Army Navy Store at 320 West Fourth Avenue (907-279-2401). In Fairbanks, there's GI Joe's Surplus at 2030 South Cushman (907-452-6225).

★ ★

In these peak years of production, the open-pit Fort Knox mine twenty-six miles northeast of Fairbanks produces about 330,000 ounces of gold annually. Like the frenzied miners of the first Fairbanks gold rush more than a century ago, Fort Knox goes after gold with a vengeance: twenty-four hours a day, seven days a week. The total estimated take from Alaska's Fort Knox? That would be a big four million ounces of gold.

Technically, Fort Knox isn't a mine, but a mill that extracts gold from the low-grade ore that comes out of a mine dubbed True North. The Canadian Kinross Gold Corporation runs the show. About a hundred miles southeast of Fort Knox, another company, Tech-Cominco, runs Pogo Mine, currently the largest gold operation in the state with estimated reserves of 5.6 million ounces.

Don't show up at Fort Knox expecting to tour and take pictures. As in olden days, the miners are a tight-lipped bunch, and only special groups are permitted to tour select parts of the operation.

Breakup
Fairbanks

It's got nothing to do with romance. In Alaska, breakup is a season, the time when you get out those breakup boots and, if you live along one of the state's many waterways, head for the river to watch—and listen—as the ice goes out.

Most flooding in Alaska happens as a result of breakup, when ice jams the river and water piles up behind it. In remote villages, a helicopter may become the only way in and out. But despite its destructive potential, breakup is mostly a time for celebration, hailing summer after a long and cold winter.

* *

FairBanks Alaska
May 8-5-1906

In this archival photo from 1906, an unnamed violinist
rides the ice during breakup in Fairbanks. A young
Fairbanks resident recently tried a similar stunt, without
the violin, but police rescue teams weren't amused.
OBYE DRISCOLL COLLECTION, 64-29-66, ARCHIVES,
UNIVERSITY OF ALASKA FAIRBANKS

Watch That Ear!

Fairbanks

A few thousand years back, naked Greeks showed off their athletic
prowess in the first Olympic Games. We've come a long way since
then: high-performance gear, complex qualifying criteria, and of
course nonstop media coverage.

For competition that's more in the spirit of the original games—but
with clothes on—Alaska has the World Eskimo-Indian Olympics, or
WEIO for short. The unique WEIO events showcase the skills needed

Seal skinning with a traditional *uluaq* during the early days of the World Eskimo-Indian Olympics
UAA-HMC-0589-3-41: ALFRED AND MAE BAKKEN SLIDES AND MEMORABILIA, ARCHIVES AND SPECIAL COLLECTIONS, CONSORTIUM LIBRARY, UNIVERSITY OF ALASKA ANCHORAGE

to survive in Alaska's harsh and demanding arctic environment. Forget humdrum stuff like the pole vault or the fifty-yard dash. The WEIO features events like the Seal Hop, the One- and Two-Foot High Kicks, and the Ear Pull.

The fun spans three days each July in Fairbanks, with contestants having trained in their home schools and towns throughout the year. Originally played on the floor of a traditional community center, or

✦ ✦

qasiq, the Seal Hop requires contestants "hop" as far as they can with all their weight on their knuckles and toes.

The High Kick events are drawn from the traditional method for announcing a harvested whale or the sighting of caribou to a village: When within sight of the community, a runner would jump, kicking one or both feet straight up, and the people would know to go to the beach to help process the meat. In the WEIO version, contestants kick either one foot or both to touch a suspended ball; in the One-Foot High Kick the height may reach that of a basketball net.

Withstanding pain is another arctic survival skill. To demonstrate that talent, there's the Ear Pull, a brutal contest in which the contestants sit facing each other, twine looped between their ears. What follows is a tug of war using ears only, with the twine making some deep cuts and blood typically shed.

These games aren't for sissies, but not every contest is so rough. There's also a seal-skinning competition, a muktuk-eating competition (muktuk, for the uninitiated, is whale blubber and skin), and a beauty pageant and blanket-toss event (see page 226), along with much good fun and fellowship.

From its origins in 1961 as a friendly competition among six traditional villages, WEIO has grown to include athletes from all over the state, but it retains the family feel of other Alaska native events, including the Athabascan Fiddle Festival in Fairbanks and the Camai Festival in Bethel.

Ghost Fort

Fort Selkirk, Yukon Territory

The town spreads out along a beautiful bend in the mighty Yukon River. Homes. Churches. Stores. A school. Over forty structures in all, vacant and abandoned but in immaculate repair.

What sets Fort Selkirk apart among ghost towns is that it's not falling down. Carefully and lovingly maintained through a joint effort of the Yukon government and the Selkirk First Nation, the town looks

Antifreeze Animals

You might wonder how our animals manage in the extreme cold of Interior Alaska. Some stay active, adapting with fur and coloration that help them get by in the snow and the cold. Even more ingenious to those of us who can only put on more layers and throw more logs on the fire are the critters who ironically "supercool" to stay warm—or the ones who literally freeze and come back to life.

Take the arctic ground squirrels, also called "parka squirrels." In winter, their body temperatures drop below freezing. Every two or three weeks, they begin to shiver and shake, warming themselves to their normal ninety-eight-degree body temperature before falling back to below freezing. It might not sound very restful, but it's a great trick for waiting out winter, and scientists believe the arctic ground squirrel's remarkable adaptation has applications in human medicine.

Then there's the darkling beetle, envy of those followers of cryogenics who scheme about freezing themselves in an attempt to cheat death. This lowly beetle doesn't just slip below freezing every so often. In extreme cold, water seeps from its cells so they can't be damaged, making it possible for the bug to hold up under temperatures as low as seventy-six degrees below zero Fahrenheit. Come spring, water returns to its cells, and it crawls away no worse off for being flash frozen.

Another bug, the red flat bark beetle, has its own ingenious method of dealing with cold, basically pumping its blood full of antifreeze. By making proteins that inhibit the formation of ice crystals, the red flat bark beetle resists freezing to a beetle-chilling 238 degrees below zero Fahrenheit, three times colder than the coldest recorded temperatures in Alaska. Overkill? Maybe. But a bug's got to do what it must to stay warm.

★ ★

almost exactly as it did when it was abandoned over fifty years ago. Step off the boat in Fort Selkirk—the river is the only road that passes this way—and you'll have the sense you've stepped back in time.

Situated below the mouth of the Pelly River, the site was inhabited for thousands of years, beginning with the Northern Tutchone tribe. Robert Campbell set up a Hudson Bay Company trading post here in 1852. Shortly after, a battle erupted with the coastal Tlingit, who had traditionally traded with the Tutchone and didn't appreciate the Hudson Bay Company stepping in. But the intruders hung on, and for nearly a century Fort Selkirk was a bustling settlement, as stern-wheelers traveling the Yukon provided the primary means of

Go in and out as you please, touching whatever you like in the old schoolhouse at Fort Selkirk.
PHOTO BY B. B. MACKENZIE

★ ★

transportation in the Canadian North. Eventually, paved highways put an end to stern-wheeler traffic, and the people of Selkirk moved to more accessible towns.

To visit Fort Selkirk is to explore the past in an independent and personal way. Visitors to Fort Selkirk must arrive by private boat or small plane. Even on a busy summer day, they're likely to encounter only a small work crew engaged in maintaining the structures. Aside from a small set of guidelines at the interpretive center, which is manned only by a television and DVD player to provide an orientation to this living museum, there's no one to tell guests where to walk or what they can and can't touch.

At Fort Selkirk it's easy to spend a whole day poking in and out of buildings, imagining what life must have been like in this northern outpost. A walking tour provides detailed information about the history of each structure and the people who lived there. At the cemeteries, you'll see colorful fenced gravesites alongside more standard markers with Christian crosses.

If you bring a tent, as many canoeing the Yukon do, you can overnight in the campground at the edge of Fort Selkirk, the campground being oddly more modern that the town itself. For a virtual tour of Fort Selkirk, visit www.virtualmuseum.ca/Exhibitions/FortSelkirk/english/index.html.

Alaska's Time Machine
Fox

Want to step back in time—say twenty-five thousand years, long before the Greeks or the Romans or the pyramids or the evidence of any human activity in North America? Alaska's got its own sort of time machine, operated and maintained by the US Army Cold Regions Research and Engineering Laboratory (CRREL) at mile 10 of the Steese Highway north of Fairbanks.

Enter the Fox Permafrost Tunnel, and you're surrounded by soils that, due to freezing, are just as they were a long, long time ago.

★ ★

Defined as ground that's frozen for at least three consecutive years, permafrost is to Alaska what sand is to the Sahara—ubiquitous and sometimes problematic. Permafrost creates all sort of interesting challenges for Alaska. We've got frost-heaved roads—drive from Tok to the Canadian border for a suspension-rattling example. Permafrost can throw a big wrench in construction plans, too. Before builders caught on, houses with basements would shift and sink as the soils underneath melted. Pilings with coolant and fins are one fix that worked to keep big sections of the Alaska pipeline from collapsing.

North of the Brooks Range, permafrost is continuous. South of there, it's found in big pockets called "discontinuous permafrost." The Permafrost Tunnel represents an old, old example of one of those pockets. It's an unassuming place, marked by only a gated driveway, a shack, and an outhouse. But from there you descend sixty-five feet through a 360-foot tunnel into a place that's frozen in time.

Originally part of a Cold War effort to test the use of underground work spaces, the permafrost tunnel has become a mecca for scientists studying everything from climate change to ancient life forms to the potential for life on other (colder) planets.

In this icy lab, researchers have discovered the teeth and bones of big mammals like mammoths and bison along with the tiny remains of Ice Age mites and butterflies. Microbiologist Richard Hoover has even managed to coax back to life bacteria that have been suspended in ice for some thirty-two thousand years.

The Fox Permafrost Tunnel exposes frozen sand, silt, and gravel as well as ice lenses, ice wedges, and an ice cave formed as permafrost melts. In the summer, it's refrigerated, and in the winter, the corps blows in air from outside to keep it frozen in time.

While the facility is now open only to prescheduled individuals and groups with a scientific purpose, an expansion project slated for completion in 2013 would include not only a new 450-foot shaft but also a learning center for visitors. In the meantime, you can step back in time with the Army Corps' video footage of the facility at www.army .mil/media/amp/?bcpid=6981683001&bctid=46866758001. You can

★ ★

also visit a smaller permafrost tunnel at the El Dorado Gold Mine (Mile 1.3 Elliott Highway; 907-479-6673; www.eldoradogoldmine.com).

Farthest North Brewery

Fox

After brewing beer in five-gallon batches at his home, Glenn Brady opened the Silver Gulch Brewery in 1988 in the historic mining community of Fox, ten miles north of Fairbanks. Today the Silver Gulch turns out beer in 750-gallon batches from a twelve-thousand-square-foot facility, including crowd pleasers like Pick Axe Porter, 40 Below Nitro, and Lowbush Cranberry Ale.

The Silver Gulch Brewing and Bottling Company grew quickly from a home-brew operation to the farthest north brewery in America.

Sunglasses and Snow

Here's an unusual must-pack item for Fairbanks in February: sunglasses. Though the subarctic is known for its short hours of daylight in winter, any Alaskan will warn you that when the sun is out, the optical effect is intense.

Sunlight bouncing off large expanses of snow can be literally blinding. You can also get "snow-burned" from the sun's rays reflected by snow. Among traditional native artifacts are sun goggles—shields for the eyes with slits carved to allow the wearer to see without all the glare.

Sun and snow work together in another significant way: They help keep the earth cool. Sunlight reflecting off the large expanses of snow in arctic and subarctic regions like Alaska is part of the world's climate-balancing mechanism—an effect known as albedo. As shifting temperatures result in the shrinking of the polar ice cap, the sun's rays are absorbed by the exposed land, which further increases warming.

Though low in the sky, the winter sun in Alaska can be blinding.
PHOTO BY G. M. FERENCY

Silver Gulch is America's farthest north brewery. Beers are brewed using Fox's famed spring water; locals without running water tap into the spring water at a roadside watering hole north of Fox. Silver Gulch beer is cold-filtered using a sophisticated German system. Processing up to 180 bottles per minute, the company's bottling plant is one of America's northernmost assembly lines, too.

In 2007, the Silver Gulch opened a popular brew-house restaurant at 2195 Old Steese Highway in Fox, in the same location as its brewing facilities.

Beyond Soldiers
Haines Junction, Yukon Territory

Quonset huts are to Alaska what quaint bungalows are in the Lower 48. Nearly as ubiquitous as moose, Quonsets dot the landscape from Barrow to Seward and from Tok to Nome. Sturdier and warmer than tents, they've served as both makeshift and permanent housing, and they've been converted to greenhouses and sheds. They're so common up here that the Anchorage Museum at Rasmuson Center not long ago featured Quonset: Metal Living for a Modern Age, a five-thousand-square-foot exhibit exploring the history and design of these portable dwellings.

Quonset huts were designed for military use during World War II. After the Japanese bombing of Pearl Harbor in 1941, the US military scrambled to take advantage of Alaska's position in the Pacific, and to defend the Aleutian chain after the Japanese invaded the islands of Attu and Kiska.

Fashioned of corrugated galvanized metal, the lightweight Quonsets could be easily shipped and assembled, making them perfect for Alaska, except for the small matter of insulation, which was often lacking. They look like pipes sliced lengthwise, with arched steel walls and two windows and a door on each end. The Quonset could be constructed on concrete where it was available or set on pilings in areas where permafrost was a problem.

Our Lady of the Way Catholic Church in Haines
Junction, a Quonset hut chapel that is still in use
PHOTO BY B. B. MACKENZIE

★ ★

Eventually the military built more permanent housing, but being portable, Quonsets continued to pop up all over the state, filling the need not only for affordable temporary housing but in some cases for schools, stores, hospitals, restaurants, and even churches. Our Lady of the Way Catholic Church at Haines Junction is one example of these alternate uses for Quonsets. In 1942, Haines Junction was a US Army supply center and construction camp for the Alaska Highway. The church was actually assembled out of Quonset hut parts in 1954. It's hard to miss—right on the Alaska Highway as you cruise through town.

Recess at Twenty Below

Those stories you tell about walking miles uphill to get to school? They'd be much more compelling had you spent your school days in Alaska, where snow days are rare and school's never cancelled simply because it's too cold. In fact, the policy at most schools throughout the state is that children will go outdoors for recess until the temperature dips past twenty degrees below zero Fahrenheit.

Since snow and cold are a way of life up here, most school cancellations have more to do with safety than with plain old winter conditions. Icy roads and ice fog so thick it's hazardous to stand at a bus stop are the most common reasons for school to be cancelled. As for recess, the rule is to bundle up and have fun.

At some schools, the Parent-Teacher Associations also sew reflective tape on students' coats so they can be easily seen walking to and from the bus stop or school in the nearly perpetually winter darkness.

As the units have aged, not as many are used for housing any
longer, but drive through almost any Alaska community and you're
likely to spot at least one. And if you really want to sleep like a soldier,
Alaska's Point of View Suites at 408 Sixth Avenue in Seward (907-
224-2424) offers two renovated Quonsets where you can spend the
night. Originally build to house USO entertainers during World War II,
the Sunshine Hut now offers weary travelers comfortable lodging and
great views of Resurrection Bay. Both the Sunshine and its sister property, the Moonshine, were used for civilian housing after the war.

The Magic Bus
Healy

There's one Alaska curiosity that gets too much attention: an old city
bus stranded in the wilderness outside the north boundary of Denali
National Park and Preserve. The bus was immortalized in Jon Krakauer's book *Into the Wild* and the Sean Penn film of the same name as
the place where the hapless adventurer Chris McCandless met his end.

Mention McCandless among Alaskans, and you're likely to evoke a
few scowls. That's because the young man trekked into the wilderness
woefully unprepared, with not much more than a bag of rice and a
rifle to sustain him. He managed to ford a river and happened upon
the abandoned bus, where he set up camp until his food ran out. By
then it was August, and the river was running far too fast and high to
cross. He died in the bus, perhaps from eating poisonous roots.

Among others, though, McCandless, who called himself "Alexander
Supertramp," is something of a folk hero, an idealist whose dreams
went tragically wrong. Drawing on an odd mix of admiration, curiosity, and plain bad sense, a few McCandless admirers have tried to
follow in his footsteps, literally, venturing to the place where he died
because—yes—he couldn't get out.

Unfortunately, foot traffic along the Stampede Trail has increased
dramatically since the release of Krakauer's book and Penn's movie.
The trek to the "magic bus"—twenty miles in, twenty miles back,

including that potentially fatal crossing of the Teklanika River—can be treacherous. Rescues have been required, and at least one person has died trying to get to the bus to see where McCandless died.

There has been talk of removing the bus, which likely got where it was when the Trail was more passable, and relocating it close to the road. Until then, our advice is to read the book, see the movie, and let sleeping buses lie.

Igloo City

Igloo City

Dreams can die slow and hard in Alaska. Twenty miles south of Cantwell, Igloo City bears witness to the slowly disintegrating dream of one entrepreneur.

Though never fully opened, Igloo City is a well-known landmark on the Parks Highway between Anchorage and Fairbanks.
PHOTO BY B. B. MACKENZIE

At mile 188.5 of the Parks Highway between Anchorage and Fairbanks sits a huge four-story igloo with dozens of dormer windows. Like many Alaska dream projects, it was ambitious: a combination motel, gas station, RV park, and souvenir shop all built in the round shape of an igloo.

The dream never fully materialized. Though the structure itself still stands, the project has long been abandoned. Windows are broken, and the grounds are unkempt. The interior was never finished, and last time we checked, the building was open to weather and vandals. It's a bit of an eyesore these days, albeit a uniquely Alaskan one.

Fannie the Hike
Kantishna

Alaska's no place for wimps, and few exemplify that better than Fannie Quigley, legendary miner, hunter, and cook of the Alaska gold fields.

From birth, life wasn't easy on Fannie. She survived a number of hardships growing up in Nebraska. At twenty-seven, a single woman alone, Fannie went north to make her fortune in the Klondike. Dragging supplies in a sled, she operated a traveling cafe near Dawson City, earning a fine reputation for her cooking and the nickname "Fannie the Hike" for her hard-working legs and her sled.

Fannie staked her own gold claim in 1900, the year she first married. But the marriage fell apart three years later, so Fannie set off alone again, hiking eight hundred miles down the Yukon River to follow the stampede as it shifted from Rampart to Tanana to Chena. Then she turned to Kantishna, a mining district in the shadow of Mount McKinley, where she staked twenty-six claims. Her Kantishna mining partner was Joe Quigley, whom she married in 1918.

In addition to working her placer claims, Fannie hunted and trapped and gardened, hauling wood and supplies by dogsled to the couple's small cabin. She dug a hole in the side of a nearby hill for storing her perishables. Her reputation for cooking, including pie crust made from

★ ★

bear lard, drew visitors from all over the mining district and the newly formed national park.

In 1930, Joe was seriously injured in a mining accident. While recuperating in Seattle, he fell in love with his nurse. He never returned to Kantishna, so Fannie lived out the rest of her life alone in the little cabin in the shadow of Mount McKinley. To see it, you have to either fly to Kantishna with one of the park concessionaires or take a park bus to where the road ends at Kantishna. The cabin's not usually open, but if you're lucky enough to get in, ask to see Fannie's "Polish contraceptive device." You won't soon forget it.

Fannie and her dogs, off for a hunt near Wonder Lake
1991-46-703, ARCHIVES, UNIVERSITY OF ALASKA FAIRBANKS

★ ★

The Way Home from Nowhere

Keno City, Yukon Territory

Looking to find your way home? The Keno Hill signpost (see photo on next page) will point the way. Capetown 10,200. Lagos 7,300. Paris 4,400. These unlikely destinations and more are marked at the top of a lonely hill outside of Keno City, elevation 3,100 feet, population twenty.

The Silver Trail veers from the Klondike Highway at Stewart Crossing toward Keno Hill, once the hub of a busy silver mining industry. In the early 1900s, horses hauled ore from the Keno mines to sternwheelers waiting in Mayo. Though active mining at Keno Hill has subsided, the United Keno Hill Mines Company hosted an international delegation of scientists during International Geophysical Year 1957–1958. Arrowed signposts point the way to the hometown of each scientist who attended.

You have to drive to the top of Keno Hill to appreciate the signpost's remote location. A winding dirt road climbs to roughly six thousand feet, giving way to spectacular views of the Ogilvie and Wernecke Mountains as well as the McQuesten Valley. A few crumbling miner's cabins dot the windswept hill, which is a good place to see alpine flora and fauna in addition to the signpost. The Beringian tundra is home to several unique species of butterflies and birds, as well as to the hoary marmot and the collared pika. Over ninety species of wildflowers bloom there each summer, and an occasional grizzly wanders the meadows.

No matter which of the signpost destinations you choose, the only way off Keno Hill is the way you came up, following the switchbacks to the tiny town with its ancient gas pump, abandoned buildings, and informative mining museum.

123

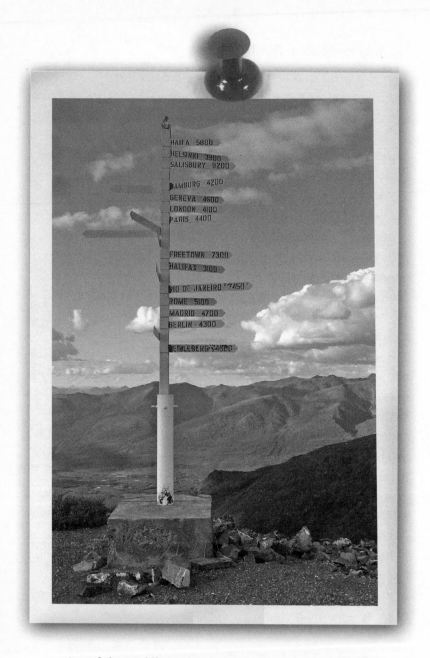

One of the world's most remote signposts, pointing the way
to cosmopolitan destinations from the top of Keno Hill

PHOTO BY G. M. FERENCY

Beer Bottle House
Keno City, Yukon Territory

If you own a hotel with a bar in a bustling but isolated mining community, you'll likely end up with a good number of empty beer bottles on your hands. One solution: Use them to insulate your house.

Old-timers used to stack bottles to make windows for their cabins, so Geordie Dobson figured they must have some insulating value. When the former merchant marine bought the Keno City Hotel in 1960, there was no refund on glass bottles, so in 1966 he began mortaring them to the outside of a house he had moved from the abandoned town of Calumet to Keno. Thirty-two thousand beer bottles

A creative and practical use for those
empties that stack up—a beer bottle house
PHOTO BY G. M. FERENCY

★ ★

later, the house is reportedly quite warm, though the effect may come as much from the mortar as from the glass.

The taciturn Dobson was quite a fixture in Keno City, once the center of a booming silver mining district. While working at nearby Elsa Mine, he rebuilt the failing Keno City Hotel, purportedly home to two ghosts. He also owned the Keno City Cafe, where he could be found smoking his pipe and challenging patrons to matches of chess. He also

Dandelion Bear

Bears love salmon. They love berries. But in the spring, fresh out of their dens, what's a bear to eat? Dandelions.

Noxious, invasive weeds that have taken over Alaska and the Yukon Territory as they have most of North America, dandelions flourish along Interior roadsides. Denali National Park and Preserve even recruits a dandelion brigade to come in at the beginning and the end of each summer season to dig the plants up by the roots and capture their seeds before they spread any farther.

The bears do their part, too, chomping on the tasty greens, oblivious to who might be watching.

A black bear chomps dandelions along the Klondike Highway north of Skagway. Black bears are distinguished from brown bears not by color but by the angles of their face and the lack of a hump between the shoulders.
PHOTO BY B. B. MACKENZIE

received an Exemplary Service Medal in honor of his work as a volunteer firefighter.

Though Elsa Mine is still active, Keno City today is a quaint and lovely home to a small community of miners and artists. Dobson has passed on, but the bottle house remains a unique attraction in a village that includes several historic buildings, including a tiny "serve yourself" library and a nice mining museum.

★ ★

Walk Right In
McCarthy

If you're patient, you can drive to one of Alaska's most picturesque little towns in the heart of the Wrangell–Saint Elias Mountains—almost.

The problem stems from the Kennicott River, a gorgeous but sometimes raging waterway that runs from the Kennicott Glacier past McCarthy to the Nizina River. During unusual periods of high glacial melting or summer rainfall, the river has taken out more than one bridge. A pedestrian tram became the only means of crossing the river, but it was dissembled in 1997 when the state built a footbridge that has (so far) held up against the current. If you want to visit McCarthy, you have to park on the other side of the river and walk across, though there is also a privately built, residents-only bridge for car and truck traffic, with access restricted to locals who buy long-term passes. If you're staying at one of the hotels in McCarthy and Kennecott, they'll likely provide transportation via this private bridge.

The footbridge is only one of the adventures awaiting those who travel to McCarthy. Built over old railroad tracks, the sixty-mile road—mostly gravel—from the Richardson Highway to McCarthy takes a good three hours to drive, and you need to keep an eye out for railroad spikes that work their way up from the road bed—they're tough on tires.

The Edgerton Highway, also called the McCarthy Road, has its share of interesting bridges, including the one-lane Kuskulana, built in 1910. Before it was repaired, the bridge was missing several planks, making it possible to view the swirling river water through the bridge as you crossed.

If you want to travel from McCarthy to the abandoned Kennecott Mine, a trip that's well worth the five-mile trek, consider bringing a bicycle over the footbridge—but keep in mind that the road between McCarthy and Kennecott is a gradually uphill incline all the way. By the way, that's not a misspelling: Kennecott, once the world's largest copper mine, is spelled differently than the Kennicott River and Glacier.

Once the pavement turns to gravel on the Edgerton Highway, you'll have to slow way down. The road is built over old railroad tracks. And once you reach the Kennicott River, you'll have to get out and walk.

PHOTO BY G. M. FERENCY

Betting on Breakup

Nenana

Spring can be a long time in coming when you live this far north. How to pass the time while you wait? Folks in Nenana had a great idea: take bets on when the ice will go out on the river.

While some jokingly name Alaska's four seasons winter, winter, winter, and winter, it's more accurate to call them winter, breakup, summer, and freeze-up. That's because so much of life in Alaska's rural communities depends on transportation that involves water. Barges run supplies up our rivers, and in winter cars and trucks use the rivers as roads. During breakup and freeze-up, transportation can grind to a halt in some places, but there's also a sense of eager anticipation about the upcoming "real" season.

Fifty-six miles south of Fairbanks, the town of Nenana perches on the confluence of the Nenana and Tanana Rivers. It's also renowned as the spot where President Warren G. Harding drove the golden spike to celebrate the completion of the Alaska Railroad, then died a few days later.

Three years before that fateful event, a group of railroad engineers who'd spent a long winter in Nenana collected eight hundred one-dollar wagers on when the ice on the Tanana River would go out. That was the start of the Nenana Ice Classic.

From that original $800 kitty, the annual proceeds from the Ice Classic now top half a million dollars. Half of the price of each ticket purchased goes to charity, and the rest goes into a jackpot that's typically split among several winners who've guessed the exact day and time, down to the minute, that the ice will first move on the river. The event is so popular that it takes a full-time manager and a couple hundred seasonal employees to run it. Tickets go on sale starting January 1 in Nenana; from February 1 to April 5, they're up for grabs to gamblers worldwide.

In Nenana, the first weekend in March is Tripod Weekend, when a tripod goes up on the river between the highway and railroad bridges.

The bridge across the Tanana River at Nenana, home of the world-famous Nenana Ice Classic
UAF-1991-46-781, ARCHIVES, UNIVERSITY OF ALASKA FAIRBANKS

(Though the newest model actually rests on four legs, everyone still calls it a tripod.) Once the tripod is set, the ice thickness is measured twice a week. When the ice starts to move, a siren sounds, and a watchman begins a twenty-four-hour-a-day vigil that typically lasts three or four days. When the tripod has traveled one hundred feet, a blade cuts the rope, stopping the clock at the official moment of breakup, and a few lucky winners find themselves several thousand dollars richer than they'd been a moment before. If you're feeling lucky, visit www.nenanaakiceclassic.com.

Santa Lives Here
North Pole

It's not the first Christmas-themed town, but geographically speaking it's the most authentic. Sixteen miles southeast of Fairbanks, the town of North Pole does its best to live up to the spirit of its name.

Santa has been around for a long time, but his home has been an official town only since 1944, when Dahl and Gaske Developments

Santa and his reindeer hang out year-round at the Santa Claus House in North Pole.
PHOTO BY KAELA TANNER

✦ ✦

subdivided a homestead and named it North Pole, in hopes that not only Santa but also toy companies would want to set up shop there. The toy companies failed to show up, but the holiday spirit lives on in North Pole, with street names like Saint Nicholas Drive, Santa Claus Lane, Kris Kringle, Blitzen, and Mistletoe.

Candy canes hang from the lampposts year-round, and Christmas colors are a favorite exterior paint choice among local businesses. Mail floods the North Pole post office each holiday season, coming from senders who want cards and packages to go out with a North Pole postmark. Letters for Santa pour in—so many that local middle school students have to help out with the answers so poor Santa doesn't wind up with writer's cramp.

North Pole's flagship attraction is Santa Claus House, founded by Con and Nellie Miller, who arrived Alaska in 1949 with only a dollar and some change in their pockets. Con started a fur-buying business, traveling to local villages where Santa loaned him a suit so he could entertain children who'd never before had a glimpse of the jolly old fellow. A few years later, one of these youngsters saw the Millers at work on their new trading post and asked if Santa was building a new house.

Sure enough, Santa moved in, and Santa Claus House (101 Saint Nicholas Drive) became one of the top retail attractions in the state. Santa hangs out there year-round. Besides posing for photos and mailing letters to children all over the world (for twenty years Santa Claus House was the town's official post office), Santa tends to the reindeer browsing out front.

The Millers' children now run Santa's House, stocking it with Christmas items (including personalized letters from Santa), toys, and Alaskana, all available for purchase. You can even buy a deed there that will make you the proud owner of a little piece of North Pole, Santa's home in Alaska.

This One Hurts
North Pole

They refine it right in North Pole, where the Alaska pipeline gleams nearby. And through that pipeline flows roughly 12 percent of the nation's oil. So why the heck does it cost so much to fill your tank in Alaska? Alaska's gasoline prices, along with Hawaii's, are generally the highest in the country. At least Hawaii's got an ocean of an excuse.

Amid suspicions of price-fixing, legislators asked that question in 2002 and again in 2008, when high gasoline prices had everyone complaining at the pump. The subsequent attorney general's gasoline

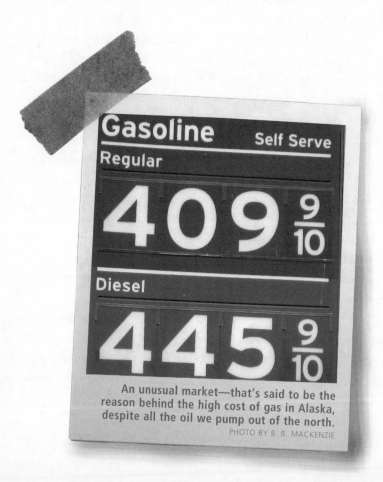

An unusual market—that's said to be the reason behind the high cost of gas in Alaska, despite all the oil we pump out of the north.

PHOTO BY B. B. MACKENZIE

★ ★

pricing report blamed it all on an "unusual market," a curiosity that Alaskans would just as soon do without.

Despite the grumbling at pumps, Alaskans keep driving. At least when prices rise beyond what consumers feel they can bear, the state sometimes suspends its eight-cent-per-gallon gasoline tax. The state coffers don't suffer: When gas prices are high, the price of Alaska crude skyrockets, too, and some 80 percent of our revenue comes from the black stuff.

The Knotty Shop
Salcha

There's no sense fighting Alaska's "state bird," the ubiquitous mosquito. Somehow, the gnarly little pests always win. So the Knotty Shop celebrates them, posing giant wooden mosquitoes on the lawn of their

A giant mosquito is among the burled wood creations on the grounds of the Knotty Shop.
PHOTO BY KAELA TANNER

★ ★

well-known gift and ice-cream emporium at 6565 Richardson Highway, thirty-two miles southeast of Fairbanks.

The mosquitoes are fashioned from burled wood, a trademark
material of the Knotty Shop. Burls form on a tree's trunks or roots as a
response to stresses such as insects or disease. These bulging deforma-
tions of the wood's natural grain can grow quite large, and while hard
to work, wood burls are prized for their uniqueness and beauty. On
the Knotty Shop lawn, you're likely to spot other wildlife, like moose,
also fashioned from burled wood.

Inside the cozy log shop you'll find an assortment of Alaska souve-
nirs, including furs, ivory, antler, pottery, clothing, jewelry, paintings,
and stained glass. For sale, too, are smaller wood products featuring
burls like those in the lawn ornaments. The shop also sells ice cream so
tasty and in portions so generous that locals will drive from Fairbanks
just for a scoop.

Here and Gone
Silver City, Yukon Territory

Tucked off the Alaska Highway, three miles down a dirt road that
branches off from milepost 1020.5 in the Kluane Lake region is Silver
City, site of a former North-West Mountie barracks, roadhouse, and
trading post that now stands abandoned. Most of the log buildings
are intact, and access of late has not been restricted.

From 1904 to 1924, wagon roads served a frenzy of mining activity in the Kluane Lake district. But as is so often the case with mining,
the rush ended almost as abruptly as it began. Wandering through the
tall grass and fireweed grown up around what was once a bustling
community, you'll see remnants of old vehicles, machinery, and even
dishes.

Because Silver City is not currently part of any park or preservation
effort, visits are at your own risk and on your own honor. On a sunny
summer day, you'll find great photo ops here.

One of several cabins in the abandoned town of Silver City

PHOTO BY G. M. FERENCY

Soapy Smith's Parlor

Skagway

He might have called it a parlor, but Soapy Smith's was nothing like Grandma's front room. Soapy's parlor was a hotbed of conning, corruption, and intimidation in the heart of Skagway during the peak of the Klondike gold rush.

The building that housed Soapy's started out as the First Bank of Skagway (at that time, spelled "Skaguay"). Jefferson Randolph Smith, aka Soapy, did a little banking of his own in the place, with most of the cash going right into his pockets.

★ ★

**Soapy Smith's parlor has seen better days—
and worse. There are now plans to restore it.**
PHOTO BY B. B. MACKENZIE

Having earned his nickname from his famous con game that duped greenhorns into paying outrageous prices for soap, Smith headed north from the silver fields of Colorado to cash in on the Klondike. The claims he staked were to power and gold, without having to go to the trouble of sluicing and panning to get it.

Soapy led a loyal gang of ne'er-do-wells who bribed politicians and law enforcement officers to look the other way as they swindled would-be prospectors fresh off the boats. One of his most notorious scams was a telegraph service operating out of his parlor. For five dollars, a clerk would take messages from the newcomers to send to the folks back home. Returning to retrieve their messages (for another five dollars), the poor saps would be invited to a poker game where they'd be convinced they held a "sure hand" that led them to lose whatever cash they had left. As for the telegraph line, it dead-ended in back of the parlor.

Skagway had a provisional government of sorts, but in 1898, the boom year of the rush, the real decisions about what went on in Skagway were made in Soapy Smith's parlor. His gang bilked count-less miners out of their life's savings, contending all the while that they were doing them a favor by leaving them enough to get home on.

Eventually the townspeople of Skagway tired of Soapy's antics, and on July 8, 1898, a shootout between Soapy and vigilante leader Frank Reid left both men dead. After Soapy's death, his partner John Clancy opened a cafe in the parlor, calling it a "gentleman's resort." Later restored as a tourist attraction, complete with a Soapy Smith effigy, the parlor eventually fell into disrepair, but it has now been acquired by the Klondike Gold Rush National Historical Park, with plans to restore the old parlor and open it to the public.

Buckwheat
Skagway

Owwwwwwwwooooooh! When you hear that call, you know he's near—Buckwheat Donahue, one of Alaska's most colorful personali-ties and champion of his hometown of Skagway. Among the most recognizable of Skagwegians, Buckwheat is the town's tourism direc-tor and general master of fun. He does a mean recitation of Robert Service and Jack London, and he hosts contests like the Belly Bump, a wintertime competition to see whose belly can bump whose off an indoor playing field. But Buckwheat has a serious side, too, involving his Heartbeat Trail walking and paddling fund-raisers.

While Buckwheat seems larger than life, in October 2003 he found himself feeling very human, suffering heart-related episodes while

Buckwheat Donahue, tourism director of Skagway and an all-around extraordinary person, worthy of the howls he shares regularly and freely
PHOTO BY B. B. MACKENZIE

passing through Juneau, Alaska's capital city, accessible only by air and ferry from Skagway. Realizing that he'd likely not have survived had the attacks occurred in Skagway, Buckwheat embarked on a project to raise money for his town's only clinic. He walked 110 miles from Skagway to Whitehorse. Then he walked 450 miles from Skagway to Dawson City. Finally in 2005 he set off on a cross-country walking tour from Alaska to Florida, all to raise money for his cause.

Buckwheat started out like a lot of Alaskans have, as a transplant from down south, gone north to work in the oil business. But his life's trajectory took a dramatic turn when he had a bit too much to drink aboard one of the Alaska state ferry vessels and slept through the docking in Juneau. A couple of Skagwegians convinced him their town was better anyhow, and after off-loading there, Buckwheat agreed. Though he had no stage experience, he started acting in the local *Days of '98* summer show, where his penchant for gold rush bard Robert Service bloomed.

Buckwheat's town has a population of about eight hundred permanent residents, but there can be as many as ten thousand people walking the streets on a big cruise-ship day in the summer. As tourism director, Buckwheat makes the little town feel like the big time, if the measure is in activities. Among other ventures, he cofounded the Yukon River Quest canoe race and the North Words Writers Symposium, and he founded the Buckwheat Ski Classic. He's hosted film crews in his kitchen, and of course he plays Santa at the community Christmas facilities.

Pick just about any fun thing to do around Skagway, and it's likely Buckwheat has had a hand in making it happen.

Brothel Tour
Skagway

The Red Onion Saloon is no ordinary bar. Built in 1897 to accommodate thirsty Klondike stampeders, it was also home to one of the classiest brothels in town.

Come in for a drink, and among the saloon's extensive collection of historic memorabilia are dolls on a shelf above the bar. In the days when this was a working brothel, each doll represented a different "girl" who worked in one of the ten-by-ten-foot "cribs" upstairs. When the girl was with a customer, the doll would be prone; when she was available, the doll was upright. A copper tube ran from each crib to the bar so the girls could deposit their earnings, which were often in gold.

The Red Onion's current employees, dolled up to resemble the working girls of the old brothel days, will be happy to escort you upstairs for a tour. There you'll see where "good time girls" like Klondike Kate, Pea

**Upstairs at the Red Onion Saloon, where
working girls plied their trade**
PHOTO BY G. M. FERENCY

Hull Annie, and Big Dessie held court. Look closely, and you might see Lydia, a former working girl said to haunt one upstairs corner.

The brothel trade dropped off in 1899, when most of the action moved north to Dawson City. In 1914, the Red Onion was pulled by a single horse from its original location at Slate and Sixth Streets to its current spot at 205 Broadway, across from Soapy Smith's parlor (see page 137). It was accidentally set down backwards, so the front and back facades had to be swapped. Before its entry into the National Historic Registry and its restoration as a saloon, the building was used as an army barracks, union hall, laundry, and bakery.

Arctic Man
Summit Lake

It's the Alaskan version of Sturgis. Or Woodstock. A winter camping and drinking and snowmachining extravaganza. (Curious fact: They're not snowmobiles here, they're snowmachines. Why? We're not sure.)

For one weekend in April, the equivalent of Alaska's fourth largest city springs up on a normally deserted stretch of the Richardson Highway in the middle of some jaw-dropping mountains. It's there that thirteen thousand people show up for the Arctic Man Classic, a unique two-day event with the motto "Go Fast or Go Home."

In Alaska backcountry spirit, the competition pairs skiers and snow-machine riders on a challenging course over the HooDoo Mountains near Summit Lake. It begins with the skier plunging 1,700 feet to the bottom of a canyon, where he latches onto the snowmachine for a two-mile tow up a second mountain at speeds topping eighty-five miles per hour. From there the skier races 1,200 feet downhill to the finish line. Times for the top contenders run an amazing four minutes plus a handful of seconds.

A Fairbanksan, Howard Thies, dreamed up this wild race back in 1985. It wasn't long before the event acquired a reputation among extreme athletes and winter-weary spectators eager to get out and party in their RVs. The former Alyeska pump station camp near Summit

Lake, leveled and cleared of buildings, serves as the state's biggest RV park for the event, with spillover all up and down the Richardson. The state troopers send a large contingent in hopes of keeping the event's extremes on the slopes without the madness spilling out among spectators. It is an exercise, as the old saying goes, in choosing your battles.

With a $25,000 prize for the top-place finishers, the Arctic Man Classic attracts top athletes of the X Games variety along with locals who know their way up and down mountains on a snowmachine and a pair of skis. Quite a few of the spectators get out and do their own riding, too, though hopefully with some caution, as avalanche danger is large at that time of year.

Galloping Glacier
Summit Lake

While most glacier ice in Alaska is receding, we have a few glaciers that get a little excited, galloping downhill at rates that may exceed one thousand feet per day. Among the best known is Alaska's galloping glacier, the Black Rapids Glacier near Summit Lake.

When advancing, glaciers normally move a few feet each year. While it's not known precisely what causes a glacier to surge, several factors are thought to contribute. Rough underlying bedrock, heightened groundwater, earthquakes, avalanches, increased seasonal snowfall—all can have the effect of a whip snapped on the back of a glacier, making it flow a whole lot faster than usual. Another likely reason for glaciers to surge is an increase in subglacial pressure caused by blocked drainage channels. In essence, this buildup of water under a glacier makes the huge ice plate slide like a hydroplaning tire on a wet roadway.

Alaska is home to more than half of the two hundred–plus surging glaciers in North America. Among the best known are Muldrow Glacier within Denali National Park and Preserve, which advanced 1,150 feet in a single day in 1936.

Then there's the Black Rapids Glacier, once clearly visible from the Richardson Highway. In 1938, it galloped two hundred feet a day

**The Black Rapids Roadhouse as it looked in 1984
after being nearly demolished by the galloping
Black Rapids Glacier almost fifty years earlier**
UAF-2003-139-145, ARCHIVES, UNIVERSITY OF ALASKA FAIRBANKS

toward the road and nearly rolled through the historic Black Rapids
Roadhouse before it finally began its retreat. Today, scientists keep a
close eye on the Black Rapids Glacier because of its proximity to the
Trans Alaska Pipeline.

Not intimidated by the prospect of a galloping glacier, new owners have opened the Lodge at Black Rapids Glacier, a timber-framed
inn near the original roadhouse, which they've stabilized to prevent its
collapse.

Soapy Smith's Wake

There's no getting around it—the people of Skagway were elated when on July 8, 1898, con man Soapy Smith (see page 137) was killed in a gun battle with local hero and vigilante Frank Reid. If you have any doubt on that matter, you need only visit Skagway's cemetery to witness the difference in markers between the two men. Reid's tomb is marked with a stately stone monument, while the slim marker for Smith, whose real name was Jefferson Randolph, leans in a forgotten corner of the graveyard.

But Smith's descendants are a fun-loving sort, and in 1974 they began the tradition of holding a wake for their most infamous ancestor. At the Eagles Lodge in Skagway at approximately 9:15 p.m. each July 8, revelers are asked to toast Soapy's ghost as they commemorate the day and the time of his death. Jeff Smith, Soapy's grandson and author of *Alias Soapy*, is among those who keep the tradition alive.

Forlorn but not forgotten, the tombstone of infamous con artist Soapy Smith
PHOTO BY B. B. MACKENZIE

✶ ✶

Mukluk Land

Tok

California's got its Disneyland; we've got our Mukluk Land, an Alaskan theme park at milepost 1317 of the Alaska Highway outside of Tok.

Part junkyard, part history, part just plain weird, Mukluk Land is definitely unique within the realm of tourist attractions. Enter by way of the big red mukluk, quite likely the world's largest. Not to be confused with whale blubber and skin (muktuk), a mukluk is a traditional boot with skin soles and fur uppers.

The giant mukluk is just the start of the fun. There are broken-down fire engines, old rusted snowmachines, dilapidated outhouses, and a giant mosquito. In short, Mukluk Land is a lot like some Alaskan backyards, except that there's also miniature golf, gold panning, whack-a-mole, skee ball, cotton candy, and an inflatable igloo.

The park was established in 1985 by George and Beth Jacobs. Like many Alaskans, George has a penchant for collectibles, aka junk. The excuse for hanging onto old hovercraft and big crawling track vehicles is that you never know when you might find a need for one—if not for the whole thing, then perhaps for its parts. Factor in the idea that there's lots of land just made for storing stuff and a strong "I'll do what I want" mentality, and you've got a uniquely Alaskan tourist attraction.

So move over, Disneyland. Cinderella may have her castle and her dainty glass slipper, but that's no competition for an inflatable igloo and a giant red mukluk.

Mud Volcanoes

Tolsona

Alaska sits on the Pacific Ring of Fire, an arc of seismically active plates that runs in a horseshoe shape from the coast of South America up the west coast of North America and across Alaska via the Aleutians to the coasts of Russia, Japan, and Southeast Asia, then down to the South Pacific and into New Zealand. The largest volcanic eruption of

147

the twentieth century occurred in 1912 at Katmai along our Aleutian chain, and 80 percent of our country's volcanoes are located right here in Alaska.

And that's not even counting the mud volcanoes, which are different beasts altogether. One batch of these unusual geological formations burbles near Mount Drum, the largest of four Wrangell Mountain peaks visible from several points along the Glenn Highway, including Glenallen. The Shrub is the largest of this group, occasionally exploding with huge quantities of mud that sputter up to thirty feet in the air. The three-hundred-foot Upper Klawasi spews a mixture of hot mud and carbon dioxide that puddles at its base, and along with the smaller Lower Klawasi, it periodically burps gas.

Unfortunately, the Mount Drum mud volcanoes aren't easy to get to, as most of the Wrangells are part of a wilderness area inaccessible by road. But if you want to get an idea of how mud bubbles up from the earth, stop at mile 173 of the Glenn Highway, where you can pay the picnic site fee at the Tolsona Wilderness Campground to hike one mile to the Tolsona Mud Springs, also known to those with some imagination as the Tolsona Mud Volcanoes. They function on the same basic principle as the more dramatic Mount Drum volcanoes, except that they belch methane and cold mud instead of carbon dioxide and hot mud. Though the Tolsona "volcanoes" aren't nearly as explosive as their more remote neighbors, it's still fun watching mud burp.

3

Southcentral Alaska

Gather up half the state's people, and you've got the population of Anchorage, the cornerstone of Southcentral Alaska. Curiously, the state's largest city began not with gold, fish, or timber like most of Alaska's first towns. It began as a tent city, chosen by President Wilson as the hub of the new Alaska Railroad, which he and others believed was the key to development in the Alaska territory. President Warren Harding drove the golden spike marking the railroad's completion in 1922. He died a few days later amid scandals and rumors that included shellfish poisoning from tainted Alaska seafood. It was not an auspicious ending for Alaska's first-ever presidential visit.

Southcentral may have gotten off to a rocky start, but it has long since made up for it. When the United States was scrambling for military presence in the Pacific after the Japanese attack at Pearl Harbor, Southcentral Alaska provided the "phantom" town of Whittier, where a secret military base was shrouded by mountains and fog. After the war, veterans settled in Southcentral's Kenai Peninsula, where there were special homesteading provisions to honor their service.

Southcentral is also known for its captivating wilderness, made accessible by the railroad that runs south from Anchorage to Seward and north to Denali and Fairbanks. Within that wilderness are fish, hoards and hoards of Russian River and Kenai reds that launch a fishing frenzy on the Kenai Peninsula each summer.

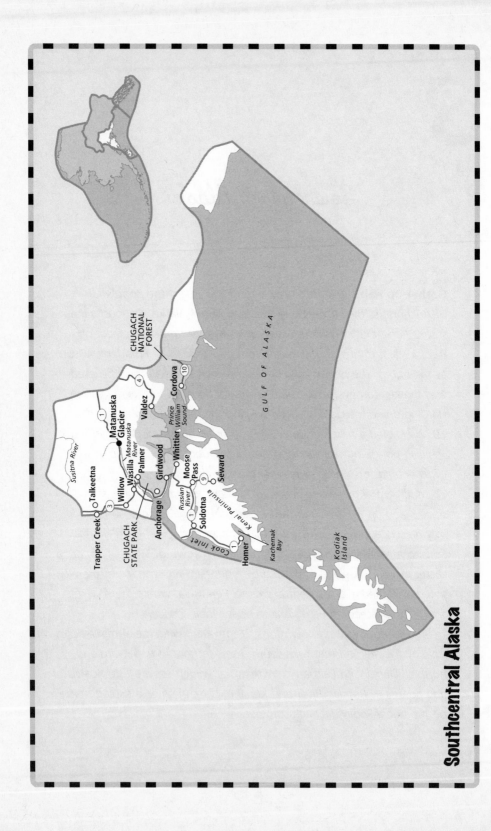

Southcentral Alaska

★ ★

Besides the railroad, the state's main highways converge on Anchorage. You can't do much better than Alaska's largest city for urban wilderness. With an abundance of parks and greenbelts on land funneled between the ocean and mountains, in Anchorage you're as likely to run into a moose on the loose as a stray dog. Downtown workers can spend their lunch hours casting for salmon in nearby Fish Creek. Bears and wolves roam nearby, sometimes wandering a little too close, proving the truth of the city's marketing slogan, "Big Wild Life."

When the North Slope oil fields opened in the 1970s, Anchorage was the hub of that activity, too. Money flowed free and easy, birthing sprawling watering holes like Chilkoot Charlie's, with its neon windmill and famous motto: "We cheat the other guy and pass the savings on to you." Anchorage was a wild and crazy place for awhile, and remnants of that spirit linger in annual events like Running with the Reindeer, where crowds gather in hopes that one of Santa's helpers will swing its antlers at a costumed runner, and the Duct Tape Ball, where any attire pieced together with duct tape is considered de rigueur.

But Southcentral's not all about Anchorage. Head north and you'll run into Wal-Mike's, Alaska's hodgepodge nose-thumbing at Wal-Mart. In Talkeetna, you can catch the annual Bachelor Auction, where you can judge for yourself the truth of the saying that when it comes to Alaska's male population, the odds are good, but the goods are odd. Paired with the Bachelor Auction: the Wilderness Woman Contest. No surprise who cobbled together that curious competition, where women chop wood, haul buckets of water, and race to their men with a sandwich and beer.

Then there's Wasilla, affectionately known as the Silla, the little town that catapulted to fame with its former mayor Sarah Palin, and nearby Palmer, where they grow cabbages as big and heady as their politicians. You can see musk oxen there, and reindeer, and stuffed dogs.

Anchorage, the Valley, the Kenai, Cordova—wherever you roam in Southcentral, the curious is in good supply. And don't worry—our shellfish is fine, too.

Fish out of Water

Anchorage

Where else but Anchorage can you leave your downtown office, pull on your waders and cast for salmon over your lunch hour? For ten days in June, you can even win big prizes playing hooky by fishing in Ship Creek, accessible by following A Street north from Third Avenue over the Government Hill Bridge. By entering the Slam'n Salm'n Derby (www.shipcreeksalmonderby.com), you can win prizes for the heaviest fish, for catching tagged fish, and for catching fish closest to the secret preselected mystery weight.

One of the salmon on parade, on display at a local hotel
PHOTO BY G. M. FERENCY

★ ★

If you lack the patience or skill for actual angling, you can still go nose to nose with wild salmon just by walking the streets of downtown Anchorage from June through August, where themed fiberglass salmon, dolled up by local artists, typically go on display as part of the Wild Salmon on Parade (www.anchorage.net/salmon), a creative fund-raising project. Working alone or in pairs, artists spin their designs from fishy puns. We've had a World Traveler fish, decked out in postage stamps from all over the world, and a Phoney Fish accessorized with mobile phones. "Spawning a Better Economy, One Spin at a Time" was the motto of the Fish Wheel of Fortune, complete with spinning game board.

Walking maps featuring the parading salmon are available at the www.anchorage.net website. After a swimmingly fine summer of display, the salmon go up for auction at a September fish fry and fund-raising event, the Fish Fry and Buy. That's when the fish migrate from Anchorage streets to local homes, with proceeds going to local charities.

Dune Town
Anchorage

It comes as a surprise when you're hiking or skiing the south end of Kincaid Park, a 1,500-acre recreational area at 9401 Raspberry Road. One minute you're in the woods, and the next minute you're facing a huge sand dune that drops down toward the ocean.

Informally named for the Jodhpur Street park entrance from which it is most accessible, the Jodhpur dune is a great place to take in sweeping views of Cook Inlet on a clear day. Dogs loving kicking up sand there, too. Accessible from a narrow trail that angles west from the Jodhpur parking lot and runs along the fence of an adjacent motocross track, the dune was likely formed during the most recent Ice Age, when glaciers crept over a hundred miles from the Chugach Mountains to the water.

The easiest approach to the trailhead is to take Dimond Boulevard west until it turns north and becomes Jodhpur Road. The Jodhpur

★ ★

On a clear day, you can see all the way down Cook Inlet from the Jodhpur sand dune. Dogs love it, too.
PHOTO BY B. B. MACKENZIE

entrance to Kincaid Park is marked with a small sign and a red gate that also serve as the entrance to the motocross track, which is open Wednesday through Sunday. In the winter, dogs are not allowed on groomed ski trails.

Ghost Tours
Anchorage

Anchorage won't be a century old until 2015, but apparently age isn't a factor when it comes to harboring ghosts. That's what Rick Goodfellow discovered when he conducted the research that led him to open Ghost Tours of Anchorage.

Take the Historic Anchorage Hotel at 330 E Street, the 1916 property that's purportedly home to not just one but to dozens of spirits—so many that the staff keeps a ghost log that includes sightings of John Blackjack Sturgis, the police chief shot by a bullet from his own gun. Also logged are reports of pictures flying from walls, presumably chucked by one or more of the ghosts.

A few blocks over at 939 West Fifth Avenue, a woman who killed herself in 1972 is said to haunt the basement restroom of the posh Hotel Captain Cook. At the Gaslight Lounge, 721 West Fourth Avenue, the jukebox turning on by itself is only one of several unexplained noises the employees say they've encountered. Even at the relatively new Anchorage Pub at Fourth and G Street, workers don't like to visit the basement alone—there's something spooky down there.

From his day job as general manager of the town's classical music station KLEF, Goodfellow dons a top hat and tails to lead nightly jaunts through Anchorage haunts. The ninety-minute Ghost Tours of Anchorage (May 15 to September 15; 907-274-4678) begin nightly at 7:30 p.m. in front of Snow City Cafe at Fourth Avenue and L Street, site of one of the most notorious murders in the town's history.

Better than the Bowl
Anchorage

It wasn't all that long ago—the 1960s—when Alaskans had no access to live television. Tapes of the Super Bowl had to be flown in after the fact, which took some of the fun out of watching.

Many years later, in 1995, the skiing women of Anchorage determined that even with live broadcasts there was still more fun to be had on Super Bowl Sunday than watching the tube and gorging on junk food. From that revelation came Ski for Women, a ski-in-costume extravaganza that attracts about 1,500 skiers of all ages and abilities who travel a four-kilometer course in heats of hundreds at a time to raise money for charity.

★ ★

A team of crayons on their way to don skis
PHOTO BY B. B. MACKENZIE

Snowy owls. Jellyfish. Cellos. M&Ms. Butterflies. Penguins. Crayons. The variety of costumes is astounding, and in some cases it's tough to determine how they manage to stay upright on skis in the garb. Contestants gather at the Kincaid Park "stadium," an open arena among the park's ski trails, at 11 a.m. every Super Bowl Sunday. A half hour later, the Grand Marshal leads a parade of all costumed entrants around the stadium so the judges can make their picks of best team and best friends or relatives costumed duo.

The race fans out from there, in several timed waves of freestyle and classic skiers. For extra bragging rights, competitors can ski the Duathlon, an 8K event that combines both classic and freestyle skiing. For the less competitive, there's the Party Wave, an untimed event skied just for fun.

Snowplow Train

Shoveling snow off the tracks of the Alaska Railroad system would take a good long time. Outside the Chugach State Park Headquarters in the former Potter Section House at mile 115.2 of the Seward Highway south of Anchorage, a nine-foot rotary snowplow train is on display. This particular plow was once used to clear snow along Turnagain Arm.

With blades that turn like a fan to cut through deep snow, the rotary plow proved more effective for Alaska's conditions than the traditional wedge snowplow, which deflects snow to the side of the tracks. Locomotives push the rotary plow, which has its own engine to rotate the blades. But due to high maintenance costs, many rotary plows like the Potter Section House model have been mothballed in favor of improved fixed-blade plows.

In addition to climbing aboard the plow train, visitors to the Potter Section House can also watch a video depicting one of the plows in action.

The vintage rotary-plow train at the Potter Section House, along the Seward Highway eleven miles south of Anchorage
PHOTO BY G. M. FERENCY

★ ★

Running of the Reindeer
Anchorage

We know Santa can make reindeer fly, but what happens when they go hoof to toe with a bunch of crazy-costumed Alaskans bent on showing their speed, agility, resilience, or just plain zaniness?

Reindeer are led up Fourth Avenue to run with a crazy costumed crowd in the annual Running of the Reindeer.
PHOTO BY G. M. FERENCY

★ ★

To discover the scientific answer to that question may or may not have been the goal of a couple of local Anchorage disc jockeys, Bob Lester and Mark Colavecchio, who proposed adding a Running of the Reindeer event to the annual Fur Rendezvous (known as Fur Rondy) festivities in Anchorage. Or perhaps they were just looking for a good laugh, which is in fact what this event delivers.

That we don't run with the bulls is a no-brainer. For one thing, they cornered that market in Pamplona, Spain. For another, bulls aren't keen on snow. And frankly, those things can get downright mean.

We Alaskans aren't dummies. Reindeer antlers may look slightly lethal, but they're relatively soft and not built for goring. Despite taunts delivered over the public address system about reindeer for breakfast, despite the wafting odor of reindeer sausage cooked on the street corner, the crazed look in the eyes of the reindeer likely has more to do with wanting to disassociate from the silly costumes around them than the good-natured goading.

Besides the usual action-hero and celebrity garb, there are always a few hardy souls who attract attention by wearing as little as possible for this outdoor winter event—men who go bare chested, women who show off fur bikinis. Fortunately, the race course is short—only a few downtown blocks—and the hundreds of racers and spectators generate their own heat. In fact, it can be tough to spot the reindeer, hemmed in as they are by the people.

But they're in the crowd, and they do run, baited by carrots and, for the males, a female in heat at the finish. If you can't be here the first weekend in March to witness this wacky event on Fourth Avenue in Anchorage, you can visit Tom Williams's Reindeer Farm in Palmer, seven miles south on the Old Glenn Highway, home of the reindeer that run with the sillies.

Whale's Revenge

Since Alaska's "One Percent for Art" program requires that a portion of the budgets for certain public works projects be allocated for art, we're blessed with lots of paintings and sculpture out in the open. But predating that program is an intriguing bronze sculpture that portrays a whale taking out a boat full of men.

The bulk of the whale, complete with realistic glass eyes, is hidden from the view of the whalers under "water" represented by a pool of bronze rings. Only the tail shows above, and it appears to have already flipped one of the boats. There's no question of who's in control: The whale is gigantic compared to the tiny men, stretching from sidewalk level to the third floor of the Carr-Gottstein building at 301 K Street in Anchorage.

The huge bronze piece, titled *The Last Blue Whale*, was sculpted by Joseph Princiotti in 1973.

Boats tipped by a whale's tail in the bronze sculpture outside the Carr-Gottstein building in downtown Anchorage

PHOTO BY B. B. MACKENZIE

★ ★

Whale Fat Is Back
Anchorage

His real name is Douglas Haggar, but everyone here knows him as Mr. Whitekeys, host and genius behind one of the most popular shows in the state: the *Whale Fat Follies*, a farcical look at life in the Far North.

The Follies opened in the summer of 1988, billed to run for only that season at Mr. Whitekeys's Fly By Night Club, a Spenard Road establishment that was easy to spot with what looked like a crashed airplane protruding from its roof. But the show ended up playing to sell-out crowds for eighteen years. After closing up shop for six years, the Whale Fat Follies are back in the same building, now the Taproot Cafe, 3300 Spenard Road, for what's again being billed as a one-season run.

Nothing is sacred at the Whale Fat. It's the best place to find Alaskans making fun of themselves—how they dress, how they talk, what they eat, and of course how they do their political business. Through song, dance, and slides, the Whale Fat gang points out that Alaska is only the forty-sixth smartest of the fifty states, but we're number two in Spam consumption (the canned meat variety) and number one in vanity license plates.

Over the years, Whitekeys's fans have sent him photos of Spam from all over the world, photos that are set to song along with the vanity plates on the Whale Fat stage. Also interspersed throughout the show are some of our state's most famous bumper stickers, like the one that says, WELCOME TO ALASKA, NOW GO HOME.

On the musical end, there's something for everyone. In a tribute sung to the woolly mammoth, Alaska's newly proclaimed state fossil, the cast ponders whether the moose nugget is the official state turd. With garish palm trees and pink flamingos flashing in the background, "Fishita" points out that the way to a man is through his fly. "Stand by Me" pays homage to combat fishing in the Kenai, while in a cover of "My Favorite Things" a lovelorn Alaskan concludes, "But then I remember he works on the Slope, and then I don't feel so bad."

161

★ ★

The Whale Fat Follies **return for a summer run
of raucous fun at the Taproot Cafe.**
PHOTO BY G. M. FERENCY

Audience volunteers take to the stage for a version of the "Blue
Danube Waltz" enhanced by the sound of ripping duct tape and conducted by an *oosik*-waving maestro. (You do recall the *oosik,* the sub-
stantial penis bone of a walrus?) There's a reverse striptease in which
the lovely lead singer dons all her man's outdoor gear, and a caution-
ary number about the temptations of wholesale shopping at Costco.
And of course no self-respecting spoof on Alaska would be complete

★ ★

without Sarah Palin belting out a rousing chorus of "I Can See Russia from Here."

In addition to providing the creative energy and pizzazz that make *Whale Fat* so popular, Whitekeys is a veteran musician and performer. During his years "off," he was in hot demand for private events and maintained a regular Friday night satirical segment on a local news show. He has also produced a DVD and a book spoofing Alaska. If you can't make it to the show, you can catch some of the fun at www .mrwhitekeys.com.

Snowless Sledding
Anchorage

Lucky for you, it's not necessary to visit Alaska in winter to experience one of our favorite pastimes—and sports—dog sledding. Though the real work of racing gets underway once the snow falls, Alaska's sled dogs train all year-round. In Southcentral Alaska, veteran Iditarod mushers Mitch and Dallas Seavey have set up a number of summer dogsledding opportunities for the curious.

The Seaveys are no strangers to dog mushing. Both father (Mitch) and son (Dallas) have run the Iditarod multiple times. Mitch won Iditarod in 2004 and Dallas has his sights set on being the youngest musher to ever win the race. Mitch is also an All-Alaska Sweepstakes champion, winning the largest cash prize in Alaska's sports history, while Dallas won the Yukon Quest, another thousand-mile sled-dog race, in 2011.

As any musher will confess, this all-consuming pastime tends to suck the whole family in, and the Seaveys are no exception. If you took in all the snowless sledding they offer, not to mention the icy glacier rides, you'd meet a lot of the Seaveys. A good starting place is the WildRide Sled Dog Rodeo at 185 East Ship Creek Avenue, where mushers and dogs compete before a live Anchorage audience. The sleds are specially designed to run on gravel, and the dogs love to pull. Every dog has his day, and one pooch in particular gets a lot of

★ ★

**Conway Seavey shows off a litter of
up-and-coming champions.**
SEAVEY KENNELS

laughs by swapping places so it's the musher pulling him around on
the sled.

If you want to do more than just watch, head two hours south of
Anchorage to Seward, where the Seaveys will take you on a two-mile
"sled" ride. Thirteen Iditarod sled dogs pull a specially designed cart
on wheels over a course that runs alongside Resurrection Mountain.

Still haven't had your fill? Swing by Girdwood, where you'll travel
by helicopter to the top of Punchbowl Glacier, where a musher and his
dog team await, ready to run you around in their endless winter ter-
rain. For details on all the Seaveys' snowless (and snow-filled) dogsledding opportunities, call (907) 224-8607 or visit www.ididaride.com.

Snowshoe Softball

Bases, bats, balls, gloves. Anyone can play softball with the standard equipment. But toss snowshoes into the mix and you've got a whole different game. Pitching and batting aren't that tough, except for a wee bit of chill in the fingers. But dashing from first base to second, chasing that fly ball—well, you try it in snowshoes.

Snowshoe softball is an annual part of the winter sports scene in Anchorage. Teams line up to compete at Kosinski Fields (Sixteenth Avenue and Cordova Street in Anchorage) on the last weekend in February as part of the Fur Rondy slate (see page 174) of events (www.furrondy .net). Regulation metal snowshoes are provided; there's no cheating with custom models. A few players even show up in costume. A good time is had by all, including the spectators, who catch a fair amount of unintentional slapstick.

A tutu can't hurt when you have to run the bases in snowshoes.
PHOTO BY G. M. FERENCY

Urban Moose
Anchorage

If you want to see moose in Alaska, don't stray far from town. Alaska's largest city—Anchorage—is home to an estimated seven hundred to one thousand moose.

During the summer, the urban moose population thins as the ungulates spread into the neighboring wilderness. But because the city is wedged between the Chugach Mountains and Cook Inlet, in the winter the moose wander mostly through city parks, neighborhood yards, and—watch out—along city streets.

It's due mostly to moose as well as the occasional bear that makes its way into the city that Anchorage uses the slogan "Big Wild Life,"

**One of hundreds of urban moose in Anchorage browses
a lawn in a neighborhood near the airport.**
PHOTO BY G. M. FERENCY

with Seymour the Moose as its mascot. For the most part, the moose don't seem to mind the attention.

However, moose can be dangerous, and many an Alaskan is more wary of them than of bears. In late May and early June when moose cows drop their calves, they become extremely territorial and will stomp anything that intrudes on their invisible boundaries.

They can also get cranky in winter, especially in heavy snow years when they have a hard time getting around and when browsing bushes and trees becomes difficult. The best practice is to give moose a wide berth and to watch their body language—twitching ears and raised hackles mean they're not happy.

In the summer, it's tough to find any way to protect a garden from moose intent on making an early harvest, and at all times of the year, it's vital for drivers to keep an eye out for moose in the roadways. The moose may not win, but a vehicle in a moose encounter will get pretty banged up, too.

For intentional moose encounters, Connor's Bog and Kincaid Park, both near the airport, are good bets. Another option is to drive west on Northern Lights Boulevard from Postmark Drive.

Snowzilla
Anchorage

What's big, white, and cold all over? Snowzilla, of course.

Anchorage gets a fair amount of snow—nearly six feet a year. The record for one winter is a whopping eleven feet. And you know the old saying: When life gives you snow, make a snowman.

That's how East Anchorage resident Billy Ray Powers sees it, anyhow. During the winter of 2005, he and his children used up most of the snow in their yard at 1556 Columbine Street on a snowman. But that wasn't enough, so they dragged snow on sleds from the neighbors' yards. By the time they were finished, a sixteen-foot snowman loomed near their house, complete with beer-bottle eyes, coal being perhaps in short supply. It wasn't long before the beast had a name: Snowzilla.

Snowzilla, hard to miss in East Anchorage
PHOTO BY G. M. FERENCY

They had so much fun they built another snow monster the following year. As it turns out, giant snowmen attract quite a crowd, and two years later, the Powerses' neighbors petitioned the city to issue a cease-and-desist order that threatened to abort the Snowzilla operation before it began.

But lo and behold, Anchorage woke Christmas Eve day to the largest Snowzilla ever: twenty-five feet. Powers claimed to have nothing to do with the creation, attributing it to holiday magic. And the city's action triggered a flurry of support in the form of Snowzilla's own website (www.snowzilla.org) featuring T-shirts, hats, and instructions for building your own personal Snowzilla.

★ ★

The scaffolding went up again on Columbine Street in January of 2011, and Snowzilla returned in his full glory. A set of barbells lies at what would be the monster's feet. This time both Powers and the city officials kept a low profile, and Snowzilla was allowed to tower over the neighborhood for yet another winter.

Wall of Water

Anchorage

When a full or new moon creates an extreme minus (low) tide, you can witness one of the world's most amazing bore tides just south of Anchorage.

At least a twenty-seven-foot difference between the high tide and the low is needed to create a bore tide—a high tide so extreme it produces a wave—in Turnagain Arm. A wall of seawater up to ten feet high rushes in from the ocean at speeds that can reach fifteen miles

A surfer rides a bore tide in Turnagain Arm
PHOTO BY G. M. FERENCY

★ ★

per hour. With the water hemmed in by mountains and the occasional seal riding in with the water, this northernmost bore tide is among the most unique of the sixty bore tides worldwide.

If you want to witness the bore tide, drive south from Anchorage along the Seward Highway. Five pullouts along the first fifty miles, including Beluga Point, offer great bore tide viewing. You may even spot a surfer trying to catch a bore tide wave, an activity that's not recommended. Be sure to watch safely from shore. Besides the extreme tidal power, the mud flats along Turnagain Arm have been known to suck people in and never let go.

Yummy Chummies
Anchorage

In Alaska, we've got fish. Lots of it. And we've got dogs. So how to bring them together?

Traditionally, salmon has been the staple fed to sled dog teams in Alaska. One species, the chum, is even called dog salmon, in part because its lower quality makes it the preferred choice for dogs. Sorry, pooches—the reds, silvers, and kings end up in our freezers.

But not every proud pet owner has access to a boat, a net, and a freezer. So an Anchorage couple invented a healthy salmon treat that could pop straight from the bag to a dog's waiting mouth. The first batches were baked in their kitchen, but now Arctic Paws manufactures the treats in a twelve-thousand-square-foot facility, producing over one million pounds of the goodies in an average year.

The Yummy Chummies product line has expanded to include salmon jerky for dogs, Crunchy Salmon, Salmon & Rice, and Salmon & Potato treats, and salmon oil that can be squirted onto dog food. In fact, Arctic Paws now claims to be the world's largest producer of wild salmon products for dogs.

If you want to bring home a special Alaska souvenir for Fido, look for Yummy Chummies at most Alaska pet and grocery stores. You can also order the tasty morsels online at www.yummychummies.com.

✦ ✦

Outhouse Obsession
Anchorage

If you have to have them, you may as well celebrate them. That's Alaska's attitude toward the ubiquitous outhouse.

We have our coffee-table outhouse collection, *Outhouses of Alaska*, and you can find outhouse Christmas ornaments at any number of gift shops. But for the really rocking outhouse fun, visit Anchorage during the February Fur Rondy (see page 174) season when the University of Alaska Engineering students host the World's Largest Outhouse Race on Fourth Avenue between E and F Streets in downtown Anchorage.

Entrants compete for honors in four divisions: Traditional, Youth, Unlimited, and Ladies of the Throne. Cash prizes are awarded to the top finisher in each category, and trophies are also handed out for the best engineered outhouse, the most colorful outhouse, the people's choice outhouse, and even—make your mother proud—the cleanest outhouse. A red lantern trophy is awarded to the last place finisher.

To race, the outhouses must be set on skis. Five-person teams race a two-lane course downtown, around a pylon and back. Riding in the outhouse must be a person sitting on a toilet seat, and the outhouse must include one roll of toilet paper. Competitors in all but the Unlimited category must enter the "shakedown" time trials in order to compete in the final rounds of the race. In the Traditional and Unlimited categories, up to two persons may pull the outhouse around the race course, while the Ladies of the Throne can have three female pushers and two male pullers in harness. A twenty-foot rope is used for pulling.

Proceeds from the World's Largest Outhouse Race send UAA students to assist with Habitat for Humanity projects. Presumably, those houses are equipped with more modern facilities. If you happen to be in Dawson City, Yukon Territory, on Canada Day (July 1), you can watch our Canadian neighbors race outhouses, too.

★ ★

Reindeer Star
Anchorage

No, it's not Rudolph, and she doesn't get to play reindeer games. But Star does have the distinction of being the reindeer mascot of Anchorage.

For over fifty years a reindeer named Star has hung out at the corner of Tenth Avenue and I Street. It's not the same reindeer—over the years there have been multiple Stars, all to the delight of Anchorage residents.

Star, reindeer mascot of Anchorage, out for a little recreation with her owner
PHOTO BY G. M. FERENCY

★ ★

The reindeer tradition began in 1960 when Oro Stewart, wife of the founder of Stewart's Photography, asked her husband for an Alaskan pet. He presented her with the first Star, a reindeer from breeder Larry Davis in Nome, so named because of the distinctive white patch on her forehead. A chain link fence in the side yard has served as Star's pen ever since.

On a leash with her current owner, Star gets out for regular walks along the park strip, and she's in hot demand for Christmas festivities and the Fur Rondy (see next page) in February. She may not still have her distinctive white star, but she's still a hit as the signature reindeer of Anchorage.

Bear Meets Shoe
Anchorage

Anchorage is home to a fair number of brown and black bears, but to see polar bears, you either have to travel hundreds of miles to Alaska's North Slope or swing over to the Anchorage Zoo at 4731 O'Malley Road. And while you'll see some lovely white bears there, it's a safe bet that none will have quite the spunk as Binky, the legendary Anchorage Zoo polar bear with a passion for shoes.

Binky became a fixture in the Anchorage Zoo not long after he was rescued from the North Slope, where he'd been orphaned in 1975. The zoo featured him prominently in their campaign to raise expansion funds for an improved polar bear habitat.

Perhaps that small bit of fame went to Binky's head, or perhaps he got tired of the crazy stunts zoo visitors occasionally pull. Whatever the reason, he made international news several years later when a tourist climbed two fences to get a polar bear close-up. Reaching through the bars, Binky made off with her shoe, and in the process, the woman ended up with a broken leg and lacerations. Having laid claim to the footwear, Binky showed off his prize for days before zoo keepers were finally able to wrestle it away from him.

★ ★

Several weeks later, some local teens decided a swim in the polar bear pool would be the ultimate adventure. They snuck into the zoo after hours, and Binky did what polar bears do when someone drops by uninvited: he attacked. Whether he took another shoe hostage in that incident has never been fully proven, but his response inspired T-shirts and bumper stickers with slogans like "Send another tourist—the last one got away."

A year after the attacks, Binky and his companion, Nuka, died of a parasitic liver ailment. Anchorage mourned his passing, tossing shoes in with his memorial flowers.

Load Your Snowballs
Anchorage

Two-hundred seventy snowballs, face guards, helmets, a fort, and a flag. Put it all together with a team of two to seven people, and you've got *Yukigassen,* a glorified snowball fight that made its US debut in the 2011 Anchorage Fur Rendezvous.

Yukigassen, or "snow battle," is a big hit in Japan, where it was started several years ago as one way to help revive a sluggish economy in Hokkaido. The 2011 Fur Rondy yukigassen tournament served as the Alaska State Championship and was also the first sanctioned event in this country.

Anchorage Fur Rondy began in 1935 as a three-day winter carnival to ease cabin fever. It grew every year until it got almost too big for its own good, with so many events spread out over so many days that attendance waned. In recent years, organizers have made a big effort to weed out the more tired events while infusing new energy with quirky competitions like sanctioned snowball fights.

One part capture the flag, one part paintball, and one part old-fashioned snowball fight, the yukigassen tournament draws a large field of pelters and flag-stealers that compete during two back-to-back weekends at a field set up on Delaney Park Strip at Tenth Avenue and G Street.

Fur Bikinis

Can't afford that fur coat? Try a fur bikini. The Anchorage Fur Factory (105 West Fourth Avenue) sells them for a fraction of the cost of a full-length fur. They're billed as fully-lined wearable lingerie, which we take to mean swimming in one is not recommended.

If you think no one would wear one of these, think again. One of the more popular contests during the annual Anchorage Fur Rondy festival (see previous entry) each February is Chilkoot Charlie's fur bikini event. Contestants sport furry tops, G-string bottoms, high heels, and not much else.

Men, don't feel left out. The Alaska Fur Factory also sells fur jock-straps that come in chinchilla, Tibetan lamb, or rabbit.

Fur G-String Bikini Size Chart

	Bust
X Small	30" (76cm)
Small	32" (81cm)
Medium	34" (86cm)
Large	36" (91cm)
X Large	38" (96cm)

A mannequin at the Anchorage Fur Factory shows off her fur bikini.
PHOTO BY B. B. MACKENZIE

★ ★

An Uphill Roll
Anchorage

You don't have to go anyplace special to roll up your sleeves or roll up a rug, but there aren't many spots where you can roll up a hill. But Anchorage has one such spot, locally known as Gravity Hill.

Fill 'er Up Alaska-Style

Alaska is not so far removed from so-called civilization that we lack the usual lazy person's conveniences. We've got drive-through fast food and ice cream and of course drive-through banking. One Anchorage hospital sometimes offers drive-through influenza vaccinations. But among drive-throughs in Alaska, coffee is king.

Alaska's not the only place where you can get your morning wake-up without leaving your car, but we've got a whole lot of drive-up espresso shops per capita. At most major Anchorage intersections, you'll find one, and sometimes two. Ditto for Fairbanks and even small towns like Soldotna and Kenai.

People who study such things say that coffee's a popular drink in the north. Alaska ranks alongside Norway and Finland for high rates of per capita coffee consumption. And when the mercury hovers near zero or lower—a lot lower, in places like Fairbanks—who wants to leave their warm car for a fix?

Folks who don't want to get out of the car in the cold can even get their brew served by bikini-clad baristas—yes, even in winter. Chalk it up to the sacrifices that must be made for a good cup of joe.

✶ ✶

To get there, follow Minnesota Drive south to where it curves into O'Malley Road. Turn right on Hillside Drive, then left on Upper Huffman. At the bottom of the first hill, turn your car around so it's pointing up where you came from, put it in neutral (watch for traffic), and prepare to be amazed as the car appears to roll up the hill.

The Espresso Simpatico Coffee Shop, a drive-through in Seward
CAROL M. HIGHSMITH'S AMERICA, LIBRARY OF CONGRESS, PRINTS AND PHOTOGRAPHS DIVISION

★ ★

It's a little unnerving to witness the reversal of a force as ubiquitous as gravity. But don't worry: Gravity is alive and well in Anchorage. The roll-up effect is nothing more than an optical illusion. The car is actually rolling downhill, but because in this spot the horizon is obstructed and the trees don't stand perfectly straight, it appears to be moving in the opposite direction.

The effect is easier to understand in the man-made version, called an Ames room, created by an ophthalmologist in 1934. While an Ames room looks square, it's actually a trapezoid, with slanted walls and tilted ceilings and floors. As on Gravity Hill, an object can appear to roll uphill there. In fact, any apparent horizon that's not actually horizontal can create the effect.

Koots

Anchorage

Like Alice down the rabbit hole, Koots is a place that just keeps getting curiouser and curiouser. From its inauspicious start in 1970 as a small Spenard bar called the Alibi Club, Chilkoot Charlie's, better known as Koots, has grown to embrace ten bars, three stages, three dance floors, and a reputation for wild, crazy fun.

After owner Mike Gordon acquired the rights to the bar's signature character, an old duffer with a gray beard and moustache and a red earflap hat, he infused the bar with Alaskan atmosphere by featuring costumed bartenders. Gordon himself occasionally showed up dressed as a World War I flying ace. Among the early entertainers was the piano-playing Mr. Whitekeys (see page 161), a well-known local performer who later opened his own Fly By Night Club down the road. Whitekeys coined Koots's famous slogan, "We cheat the other guy and pass the savings on to you."

You never know who or what you'll run into as you wander Koots's sawdust-covered floor through the maze of themed rooms. In the Swing Bar, there are old black-and-white films to be enjoyed with special Koots martinis. The Russian Room features relics from the country

"We cheat the other guy and pass the savings on to you"—that's the motto at Koots.
PHOTO BY B. B. MACKENZIE

we can almost see from here—but not quite. Another favorite is the Bird House Bar, a replica of a popular hangout between Anchorage and Girdwood that was destroyed by fire several years back. Lingerie suspended from the ceiling, boneless chicken dinners, and ptarmigan whistles (you'll have to ask) are among the attractions.

★ ★

Koots draws big name bands, and it has received tons of press acclaim. After being named Number One Bar in America by *Playboy* magazine in 2000, Koots's owner presented Hugh Hefner with an *oosik,* a bone from a male walrus that is substantially larger than what one might think would be needed to make baby walruses. Hefner's response, in a letter displayed on the wall of one of Koots's many nooks, admits a walrus might be a hard act to follow.

Odd, quirky, and a rollicking good time, Koots is easy to find. Look for the giant lit windmill at the corner of Spenard Road and Fireweed Lane.

Duct Tape Ball
Anchorage

Roll out the carpet, put on those dancing shoes, and grab a roll of duct tape, the ubiquitous fix-all staple of life in Alaska. Each winter in Anchorage, community-minded revelers dress to the nines for a black tie and duct tape event that is also a big charity fund-raiser.

The idea for a duct tape ball was generated in 1998 among several friends sitting around a campfire. With duct tape tacking together Alaska necessities like luggage and small planes, they came up with the idea for a spec-"tack"-ular event in which duct tape would be part of the dress code

The annual Duct Tape Ball features all sorts of wacky and wild duct tape creations. There are duct tape bow ties and miniskirts, as well as duct tape hats, gowns, and vests. Duct tape divas flaunt tacky boots and sticky camisoles. Room decor has included duct tape cars, a duct tape pirate ship, a ten-foot duct tape giraffe, and a hundred-pound duct tape gorilla.

Over the years, the Duct Tape Ball has acquired several sponsors, including—you guessed it—Sure Tech, makers of Duck Brand Duct Tape. All proceeds from the ball benefit local charities, with over a million dollars raised in the first eleven years of the event's history.

★ ★

Downtown Dogs

Anchorage

Most northern cities budget for snow removal, clearing their streets for traffic in winter. But in Anchorage, we budget for the occasional snow dump, hauling in white stuff for special events, most of which involve dogs.

After being scooped off the streets and delivered to the Anchorage snow dump, snow is returned to downtown streets for events like the start of the Iditarod Sled Dog Race on Fourth Avenue.
PHOTO BY G. M. FERENCY

★ ★

It starts with the Fur Rondy (see page 174) sprint races in late February each year. The twenty-five-mile course runs from Fourth Avenue at D Street down Cordova Hill through midtown to Far North Bicentennial Park, where the sled-dog teams run on actual trails before returning downtown. Teams travel from all over the world to compete in this International Sled Dog Racing Association event. Since asphalt isn't ideal for mushing, crews haul in snow to cover the roadways, then scoop it out when the three days of racing are finished.

Among the best places to view these "downtown dogs" is on Fourth Avenue when the race starts at high noon each day. Other popular viewing spots include the intersection of Cordova Street and Sixteenth Street, Woodside Park on East Twentieth Avenue, Goose Lake Park off University Avenue, Tudor Road between Elmore Road and Boniface Parkway, and Campbell Airstrip Road near Benny Benson School.

More snow is hauled in to cover downtown streets for the ceremonial start of the Iditarod Sled Dog Race at 10 a.m. on the first Saturday in March. The teams follow a similar course, encouraged by much cheering and hoopla, ending their runs at the Campbell Creek Science Center. From there they travel forty-nine miles by truck for the real start in Willow at 2 p.m. the following day.

Before the Iditarod snow is hauled out, it gets one more trampling in the Fur Rondy Running of the Reindeer event (see page 158), held at 4 p.m. on the same day as the Iditarod ceremonial start.

The Dome
Anchorage

It's a hard-to-miss and puzzling Anchorage landmark off the intersection of well-trafficked Minnesota Drive and Raspberry Road: a gigantic white, poofy dome with mountains behind in the distance. Known locally as "the Dome" and officially as the Alaska Dome, it's the largest air-supported structure in all of North America. An off-shoot of nearby Changepoint Church, the Dome is open for fee-based public use.

★ ★

The Alaska Dome, the largest air-supported structure in North America, allows sports enthusiasts to extend their seasons.
PHOTO BY B. B. MACKENZIE

Measuring 601 feet long, 290 feet wide, and 87 feet high, the Dome is well-suited for meeting its goal of transforming the Alaska athletic experience, which in winter is a challenge for nonsnow sports. Football, rugby, soccer, kickball, softball, baseball—all get play time in the Dome, where it's never winter inside. There are also batting cages, showers, and a track for individual running and walking.

Mud Transformed
Anchorage

The first lesson you learn about Cook Inlet mud: Stay away. The stuff that lines the shores of the inlet near Anchorage can be worse than quicksand, sucking in unsuspecting hikers, which creates a huge hazard when combined with the inlet's tides, some of the strongest on the planet.

But one Anchorage engineer has found a way to tame the treacherous slop. Harvesting it with care, he transforms Cook Inlet mud into tiles that he imprints with unique natural images, some of them reflecting his Inupiaq heritage. After discovering his passion for printmaking and tiles, Ed Mighell quit his day job to devote himself to his craft. He dries glacial-silt clay, crushes it between rollers, and reconstitutes it with water, mixing in minerals to strengthen it so that it can withstand the high temperatures of the kiln.

Before he fires his creations, Mighell carves, etches, and presses designs into the tiles. Using white, black, and earth tones of red, he paints loons, ravens, and caribou with strong, stylized lines. On some tiles, he colors impressions made from leaves representing Alaska's familiar trees—birch, popular, and aspen.

Mighell has discovered that people like mud, at least once he's worked his magic with it. He sells his tiles at the Anchorage Weekend Market at Third Avenue between C and E Streets, the Alaska Native Heritage Center at 8800 Heritage Center Drive, and the Anchorage Museum at Rasmuson Center at 625 C Street.

★ ★

Zapped Bear

Anchorage

Anchorage boasts more urban wildlife than most other cities. Moose wander through yards and along roadways, and it's not uncommon for black bear to be tucked away in the parks near the Chugach Mountains, the range that runs along the east side of the municipality, mostly minding their own business.

For the most part, residents use good sense when encountering big mammals like bear, and for the most part, the bears use good sense, too. But the occasional one gets into trouble, like the brown bear that dug into an electrical box along the Tony Knowles Coastal Trail and ended up, well, fried.

In August of 2006, a child riding her bike along the eleven-mile Coastal Trail, one of the most popular recreational spots in the city, happened upon the zapped bear. Wildlife officials speculated that the bruin had either come up from a wilderness area south of Anchorage or had swum across the inlet. Apparently bears are like cats, curious about their environment, but with a lot more power when it comes to investigating. And apparently they have a penchant for plastic.

The seven-foot bear ripped into the box and bit into a large electrical wire, charring its tongue and teeth. The grass under its foot was also burned. Perhaps word got out among Anchorage wildlife; since then electrical boxes have gone unchallenged by bears.

Alaskan Elephant

Anchorage

When it comes to well-known Alaskan mammals, you wouldn't think first of an elephant. But for nearly twenty-five years, visitors flocked to the Alaska Zoo to see Maggie, Alaska's famous elephant.

It all began in 1966 when a local grocer won a contest in which the prize was either $3,000 or an elephant. He chose the elephant, naming her Annabelle. But Anchorage wasn't exactly set up for housing an

★ ★

elephant, and so he ended up transferring his prize to the owner of the Diamond H Horse Ranch, the only facility with heated stalls.

Word got out about Annabelle, and as people flocked to see her, the horse-ranch owner led a community effort that resulted in the con-struction of Alaska's first zoo. Annabelle continued to be a star attrac-tion, but her keepers feared she was lonely, so in 1983, they acquired a young female named Maggie to keep her company.

Until Annabelle died in 1997, the two elephants braved Alaska's winters together—in heated enclosures, of course. They even created some elephant art, painting with their trunks. But once Annabelle was gone, Maggie appeared lonely and bored. She acquired a reputation for crankiness, which many said was no fault of her own. A "Free Maggie" movement began. There were bumper stickers. Letters to the editor of the local newspaper. Testimony given before the Anchorage Zoo Board of Directors. Maggie became one of the community's hot-button topics

The zoo's board remained convinced Maggie belonged there. To counter her boredom, zookeepers suspended her hay in the air so she'd have to work for her food. They even designed a one-of-a-kind elephant treadmill so Maggie could exercise. As seems the way with treadmills, Maggie used it once and then ignored it.

One day in 2007, Maggie collapsed and couldn't get up. Paramed-ics had to use a crane to get the eight-thousand-pound elephant back on her feet. Television celebrity and animal-rights activist Bob Barker flew to Alaska on behalf of the Performing Animals Welfare Society (PAWS). He extended an offer from PAWS to fly Maggie to California, where she could roam on a hundred-acre preserve in the company of other elephants.

After some deliberation, the zoo accepted the offer. It took months of preparation and training, including coordination with Elmendorf Air Force Base, but one day Maggie strolled into an eighteen-foot cargo container and rolled away from the Alaska Zoo in a flatbed truck that took her to an Air Force cargo jet for the flight south. "Operation

**Maggie in her compound at the Alaska Zoo,
a few weeks before her move south.**
PHOTO BY B. B. MACKENZIE

Skate on a Pole

You'd think in Alaska our fetish would be for skates with blades, but the biggest skate in the state is on wheels. The giant skate tops a pole outside Skateland, a roller rink at 8100 South Seward Highway, north of Dimond Boulevard in Anchorage.

Skateland has been around since the 1970s. Before that, the giant skate topped Anchorage Roller Rink. The same owners operated both facilities for many years before they closed Anchorage Roller in the mid-1980s and relocated the giant skate to its current home outside Skateland. In keeping with the theme of big stuff, one inside wall of the rink is painted with a mural of Mount McKinley, the highest peak in North America. Anchorage doesn't have the only giant skate in the nation. Big shoes on wheels can also be found in Virginia, Florida, Georgia, and South Carolina.

As for roller rinks, Skateland is holding its own in Anchorage,

Where's the blade? Giant skate on a pole, an Anchorage landmark outside Skateland
PHOTO BY G. M. FERENCY

though ice-skating rinks get more use by far. In North Pole, the only roller-skating rink in the Interior was converted several years ago to ice in order to meet the demand of local hockey leagues and figure-skating clubs.

Maggie Migration" was underway. Her journey was the lead news story as Anchorage residents tracked her progress toward her new home.

It didn't take Maggie long to adjust to the California sunshine. Alaskans still watch her by webcam at www.pawsweb.org.

Shamed

Cordova

What's the best way to let the world know that someone has done you wrong? There's country music, but the more Alaskan solution is to carve a shame pole.

Alaska's Tlingit, Haida, and Eyak are renowned for carving colorful totem poles. Most tell stories or commemorate special events, but poles have also been carved to draw attention to public transgressions.

One of the biggest public transgressions to hit Southcentral's Prince William Sound was the huge 1989 oil spill caused when the tanker *Exxon Valdez* ran aground at Bligh Reef in the sound. So it was only fitting that on the eighteenth anniversary of the infamous *Exxon Valdez* oil spill in Prince William Sound, the Native Eyak village of Cordova erected a pole commissioned to shame Exxon for what it considered insufficient compensation for the Alaskans who'd lost their livelihoods as a result of the spill.

Carved by Mike Webber, an Eyak tribal member whose way of life was forever changed the day the *Exxon Valdez* ran aground, the pole is a seven-foot reminder of damage done and promises broken. Represented along the length of the pole are dollar signs next to the words "We will make you whole," as well as lady justice and a notice reading "past due," a reference to the long court delays associated with settling claims in amounts that many say are insultingly low.

The shame pole stands outside the Ilanka Cultural Center at 100 Nicholoff Way in Cordova, which like Valdez was hit hard by the effects of the Exxon spill. The center honors the cultures of the Eyak, Alutiq, Tlingit, and Ahtna people of Alaska.

★ ★

Surf's Up . . . North
Cordova

So maybe it's not the first place that comes to mind when you think of surfing, but Alaska has its own small mecca where die-hards cruise the waves on the northernmost part of the Pacific Ocean despite water temperatures that average fifty degrees Fahrenheit.

The Alaska advantage: hundreds of miles of rugged coastline with virgin breaks yet to be surfed. The backdrop, too, is unique: the Wrangell Mountains, boasting some of the state's tallest peaks. These surfing beaches, uncrowded by any standards, are a forty-minute boat ride from Cordova, or fifteen minutes by air. Points North Heli-Adventures of Cordova (877-787-6784; www.alaskaheliski.com) offers excursions to the breaks in the form of either day trips or overnight stays.

Surfing conditions are a little different in the Far North, and if you want a custom board to ride the waves here, you can get one at AK Surfboards (877-787-6784) in Cordova. A wet suit is a wise investment as well.

Nearby (per Alaska standards) Yakutat has been named one of the five best surf towns in the United States according to *Outside* magazine. Yakutat's not exactly crawling with surfers—there might be a couple dozen or so out of the town's eight hundred residents. Still, it calls itself "Surf City, Alaska." But Cordova's not worried—there's plenty of ocean to go around.

Million Dollar Bridge
Cordova

You've likely heard the flap about Alaska's Bridge to Nowhere (see page 27), poster project for wasteful government spending schemes. But while the Bridge to Nowhere never got past the planning stages, Cordova's "Million Dollar Bridge" has been around for over a century.

A million dollars might seem like a bridge bargain these days, but back in 1910 when the Cordova project was completed, it was quite a

The CRNW railway "Million Dollar Bridge" over the Copper River near Cordova. Steel rails and steel girders are shown in perspective. The bridge is officially known as the Miles Glacier Bridge.

chunk of change. And in the fine tradition of cost overruns, the actual cost of the 1,550-foot steel structure was $1.4 million.

The bridge was built for the Copper River and Northwestern Railway, dubbed the "Can't Run and Never Will" railroad by its detractors. The CRNW was the winner of a high-stakes, sometimes violent battle involving wealthy East Coast investors like the Rockefellers and the Guggenheims over who would provide rail service to the Kennecott Copper Mine, which at that time held the world's largest supply of copper, a metal coveted during an era of industrial expansion.

Low copper prices forced the mine's closure in 1938, and the railroad shut down. In Alaska's 1964 Good Friday earthquake, the northern span of the Million Dollar Bridge dropped into the river. End of the story you might think, but you'd be wrong.

Rather than face a costly environmental cleanup if the whole bridge collapsed into the water, it was determined more prudent to repair the broken end. So the bridge was fixed, even though the road that crosses it dead-ends on the other side. From the small town of Cordova, accessible only by water and air, you can still drive fifty miles to cross the Million Dollar Bridge, take in a spectacular view of Childs Glacier, then turn around and come back, because this expensive steel structure leads nowhere.

Hooligan
Girdwood

If you drive south on the Seward Highway in the late spring, you'll need to allow a little extra time on account of the hooligan. Cars line the roadsides, anglers with waders and nets clomp toward the water, wielding nets, and temporary speed limit signs force a slowdown. All this commotion results from a skinny little fish that runs like crazy in the spring.

Hooligan, also known as smelt, were once a staple of Alaskan life. The Tlingit and other Alaska native people traditionally dried these small, oily fish and strung them with wicks made from spruce bark. Used as candles, the fish were also called candlefish.

Alaska natives rendered hooligan oil, too, storing it in jars fashioned of kelp bulbs for trading with Interior Indians who had no access to the fish. This trade was so significant that the routes used came to be known as "grease trails." The oil is a diet staple, used like a sauce for dipping other traditional food, the way seal oil is used by Yup'it and Inupiat who live along Alaska's western and northern coasts .

Hooligan can only be dipnetted during a short spring season when the nine-inch fish run in hoards from saltwater to freshwater to spawn. They aren't strong swimmers, so they rely on the tide to push them upstream. The delicate flesh is best eaten or frozen soon after the fish leaves the water. It may also be pickled to firm and preserve it.

Salty Dawg Saloon
Homer

History takes some strange forms in our state, as demonstrated by the venerable Salty Dawg Saloon on the Homer Spit.

The Salty Dawg opened in 1957 in a log cabin, dating back to 1897, that was once a post office and schoolhouse. Another cabin was added, and the whole compound had to be moved after it was nearly washed into the sea during the 1964 Good Friday earthquake. Its lighthouse came later, built to conceal a large tank that holds drinking water. It's one of the landmarks on Homer Spit, which rivals "downtown" Homer for action. Fishing charters, fish shops, retail shops, restaurants, informal camping—it all comes to life in the summer along this narrow finger of rock and sand that juts into the ocean.

Ducking into the Salty Dawg is like slipping back in time. From the dollar bills that plaster the ceiling to the license plates and notes on the walls, it seems every previous patron has left some sort of mark there. With no seeming worries about identity theft, people have even tacked up their driver's licenses and ID cards.

Most leave with some sort of souvenir, too. Salty Dawg T-shirts and sweatshirts make up a good deal of Alaska's summer attire. In Homer, it's the place to be and to say that you've been.

The Salty Dawg Saloon on the Homer Spit
PHOTO BY B. B. MACKENZIE

Larger than Life

Along the east side of the Sterling Highway as you near Homer, this giant mosquito, a larger-than-life replica of Alaska's "state bird," greets you. Though by its annoying persistence the mosquito steals a lot of attention, Alaska's real state bird is the ptarmigan.

A big bad mosquito along the Sterling Highway
PHOTO BY GAIL GILES

★ ★

Combat Fishing
Kenai

Fishing in Alaska. The image that likely comes to mind involves standing alone on a remote river, surrounded by mountains, drinking in the quiet, pulling up a fish every other cast. There are plenty of Alaskan

Bear Makeover

In nature, bears come in neutral shades—brown, black, and white. But a few summers ago, a big makeover recolored some Russian River bears in colorful shades like orange and hot pink.

The makeover program was one attempt to cut down on what the Alaska Department of Fish and Game calls "negative bear-human interactions." The Russian River is a popular spot for sport anglers fishing for salmon, which are a tasty treat for bears as well as humans. When anglers get sloppy and leave out their food, trash, or stringers of fish, bears quickly learn that a little intimidation will yield an easy meal.

State wildlife troopers began tranquilizing the problem bears. Once under, the bears got the full salon treatment: a shampoo and dye job. The concept was that bears with atypical coloring would stand out, and humans would know to stay clear of them.

The program met with some success, but there were also complaints that stumbling on a hot pink bear didn't jibe with the Alaska wilderness experience, and the bears may not have been crazy about the forced makeovers either. The long-term solution involves not so much branding bears as educating humans to be more careful with their food and their fish.

★ ★

places to play out that dream, but if you want to fish like a real Alaskan, a curious experience awaits: combat fishing.

It may not exactly be anyone's dream, but combat fishing is the way it's done on a lot of the Kenai Peninsula. At the peak of a salmon run there, you might share your great fishing hole with, oh, a thousand or so other anglers. That sort of coziness requires some defensive tactics to make sure you don't end up hooking your neighbor—or accidentally baiting a bear.

Fortunately, there are plenty of fish to go around. King Salmon? Figure seventeen thousand or so in an average season. Silvers? Maybe forty thousand. Reds? Believe it or not, a million red salmon can charge up the Russian and Kenai Rivers in a good year. No wonder anglers are willing to layer themselves shoulder to shoulder to catch their limits.

A boat, plus a change of seasons, makes for more relaxed fishing in the Kenai Peninsula.
PHOTO BY G. M. FERENCY

To take your turn combat fishing, line up along the Kenai River just south of Cooper Landing and wait for a spot to open up. It may be combat, but it's considered bad form to elbow your way in. Worse than bad form, it's dangerous to slide in behind someone who's casting.

Once you acquire a spot in the front lines, try to time your cast with the anglers nearby. Holler "fish on" when you've hooked one so that others can get out of the way. Land it quickly so you don't tangle lines with anyone else. If you snag a fish, break the line instead of trying to play it. And once you've caught your limit, step aside and let someone else step up for their combat duty.

If you want to see what happens when you don't abide by the combat fishing rules of engagement, stop by the Central Peninsula Community Hospital in Soldotna; in the emergency room there are a couple of mannequins stuck with actual lures in the same spots from which they were extracted from the flesh of very real people. On average, the staff retrieves two hundred lures for their showcase every season.

Rock Glacier
Matanuska Glacier

It looks like a beard trailing down the side of the mountain, but it's actually a glacier—a rock glacier. These rare glaciers form only in places cold enough to sustain permafrost, and while that means much of Alaska, it's not all that often you'll see one up here, either.

One easy place to spot a rock glacier is traveling west on the Glenn Highway, between mile 101 and mile 100, near the small community of Glacier View about thirty miles east of Sutton. To the right, in Anthracite Range, a big rock glacier runs down a mountainside. You can also get a look at this rock glacier from the Matanuska Glacier State Recreation Site at mile 101 of the Glenn Highway. An interpretive sign points it out.

Rock glaciers are actually hybrids, containing both rock and ice. Though scientists aren't sure how they form, they do know they're able to maintain their own microclimates, so even in the summer when

A rock glacier on Anthracite Ridge near mile 100 of the Glenn Highway
PHOTO BY G. M. FERENCY

the sun heats the dark rock, the ice underneath doesn't melt. While glacier ice behaves like water and is therefore said to "flow," rock glaciers are said to "creep." Without getting up close, it's hard to tell where the glacier ends and the moraine begins, as the rocky surface looks similar for both.

If you're up for a hike, you can get even closer to a rock glacier by following the Rock Glacier Trail in Kluane National Park and Reserve, Yukon Territory. The trailhead lies thirty-one miles south of Haines Junction, in a pullout off the Haines Highway. Though the looped route is only 2.1 miles, it's mostly uphill, so it's wise to allow two hours to complete the hike, which leads to a viewing platform at the toe of a rock glacier.

Armed Bear
Matanuska Glacier

At mile 102 of the Glenn Highway, you'll likely have a hard time taking your eyes off the spectacular Matanuska Glacier, winding twenty-seven miles into the Chugach Mountains. But if you look away for a moment, you'll spot a rooftop bear standing guard with a rifle.

An armed bear stands watch from the roof of the Long Rifle Lodge.
PHOTO BY G. M. FERENCY

In this area, an unincorporated community known as Glacier View has an active muzzle-loading club, and the bear tops the aptly named Long Rifle Lodge. Built in 1975, the lodge offers dining with amazing views of the glacier under the watchful eyes of one of the biggest collections of taxidermied animals you're likely to find anywhere. Stop by around Halloween, and every one of them will be costumed. Besides the weatherproof bear on the roof of the lodge, there's a big stuffed one that will keep you company at the bar.

Also on display at the Long Rifle are antique mining equipment and some of the fossils for which this area is known. The friendly owners serve a mean bowl of chili, voted best in the state by the *Washington Post,* along with a complete breakfast, lunch, and dinner menu. The tables and chairs are handcrafted from logs, and there's also counter seating where the locals gather to hash over the latest news.

The Long Rifle rents rooms in the summer and dry cabins in the winter. They are also concessionaires for the nearby Matanuska State Recreation Site, where there are interpretative kiosks for the glacier, a well-marked nature trail, a nice campground, and a state park service cabin that can be rented by the night. For details, call the Long Rifle at (907) 745-5151.

Matanuska Megafloods
Matanuska River

Ice dams do a lot of damage in Alaska. Along the Yukon and Kuskokwim, the state's two largest rivers, residents watch anxiously each spring as the ice goes out. While the rush toward springtime is welcome, everyone hopes the ice won't jam up in their part of the river and cause catastrophic flooding the way the Kuskokwim did in Cripple Creek during May of 2011.

As devastating as modern ice dams can be, nothing compares to the megaflood that scientists believe resulted when an ice dam broke some seventeen thousand years ago. According to a report released by the University of Washington and published in the journal *Quaternary*

The Cathedral Cliffs along the Matanuska River show how much sand was released by the Matanuska megaflood.
PHOTO BY G. M. FERENCY

Research, the collapse of the ice sent water rushing from a gigantic glacial lake toward the coastal area where Anchorage now lies at the rate of some three million cubic meters per second.

The ancient lake that drained with such force was a 3,500-square-mile whopper named Atna. Beyond the initial break, its waters spilled from the Copper River Basin through the Matanuska Valley in a series of megafloods that left some parts of Southcentral Alaska under five miles of water. As the water drained, it formed sand dunes over one hundred feet high.

Much of the sand was dumped in the Anchorage area, leaving a layer of sediment that proved unstable during the famous 1964 Good Friday earthquake, when the top layer of earth slid from the liquefied layer, dumping homes and other structures into the ocean in the coastal area now set aside as Earthquake Park. Later studies revealed that some of the unstable earth was infused with freshwater, an unlikely occurrence so close to the ocean. The ice dams, and the floods that resulted, are to blame.

One of the key pieces of evidence for the megaflood, deemed one of the largest ever in the world, is the pygmy whitefish, which Alaska researcher Michael Weidner discovered in mostly fishless Lake George. Close cousins of the little guy were found in other mountain lakes once within Atna's reach, affirming the theory that the freshwater flood was extensive.

An Axe to Grind
Moose Pass

Have an axe to grind? The fine people of Moose Pass invite you to use their working waterwheel, free of charge.

This little gem of a town lies along the Seward Highway, one hundred miles south of Anchorage and thirty miles north of Seward. Named for an abundance of moose in the area back when the Iditarod Trail connected the seaport of Seward with faraway Nome, Moose Pass has seen its heyday come and go. Only two hundred residents now call the town home, but for years after the community was founded in 1909 as a supply post for gold miners, it was a center of transportation, mining, and logging.

Among the early residents of Moose Pass was the Estes family, who installed a waterwheel in 1927 to power their sawmill. Leora Estes Roycroft was the postmaster who named the town the following year. Until 1956, the waterwheel supplied power not only to the sawmill but also to the town site.

A replica of the Moose Pass waterwheel turns along
the side of the Seward Highway at Moose Pass.
PHOTO BY G. M. FERENCY

✦ ✦

In 1980, the current ten-foot-high replica of the functioning water-wheel was constructed. It runs a stone, also a replica of the original, on which knives and axes can be sharpened.

A Whole Lot of Coleslaw
Palmer

Alaska isn't exactly known for its farm country, but we do have one claim to fame when it comes to tilling the soil: monster-sized vegetables. Though our growing season is short, the extended hours of summer daylight yield all sorts of world's record vegetables, especially among the varieties that do well in cool soils.

In late August and early September, thousands of visitors flock to the Alaska State Fair in Palmer to check out the supersize veggies. In 2009, there was Steve Hubacek's world-record cabbage. Weighing in at 127 pounds and with leaves that spanned five feet, the cabbage was so big that it took several men to wrestle it from the truck to the judging area. Hubacek, who has been growing big cabbages for several years, was awarded a $2,000 prize. While you might think he also grew himself a winter's supply of coleslaw, the truth is that oversized vegetables don't make the best eating.

That doesn't stop farmers from aiming for the record books. Among the giants, Alaskans have produced a 19.98-pound carrot, a 28.75-pound kale, a 59-pound zucchini, a 39.5-pound kohlrabi, a 42.75-pound beet, and a 35-pound broccoli.

Though Alaska's earliest settlers raised much of their own food, it was in the 1930s that there was a big agricultural experiment here. As part of Roosevelt's New Deal, the federal government transported dozens of farm families from Minnesota and Wisconsin to the Matanuska-Susitna Valley, where conditions proved ideal for big vegetables but, as it turned out, not for big-scale agriculture.

Descendants of the original Mat-Su colonists remain in the valley to this day. A few have maintained their homesteaded acreage, while

★ ★

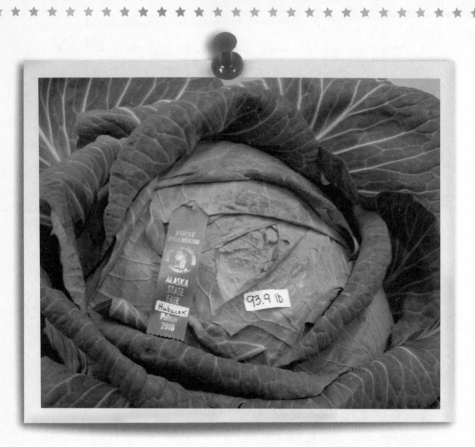

**It takes a big cabbage to win a blue ribbon
at the Alaska State Fair in Palmer.**
PHOTO BY G. M. FERENCY

others have sold out to developers in the fast-growing bedroom communities of Wasilla and Palmer. Today, small farmers from the valley
supply high-quality produce to local restaurants, and farmers' markets
offer an opportunity for locals to purchase fresh vegetables of more
ordinary proportions than what you see at the fair. Valley potatoes and
carrots are huge favorites, prized for their sweetness, but you'll find
lots of other produce as well at the weekend Anchorage Downtown
Market on Third Avenue between C and E Streets. In Palmer, there's
the Friday Fling market at the pavilion across from the visitor center,
and the Wasilla Market behind the library is open on Wednesday.

★ ★

Most Alaska farmers' markets are open seasonally from May to September. For more information on where to buy Alaskan produce large and small, visit www.alaskafarmersmarkets.org.

Ice Worms
Portage Valley

Worms that live on the ice? It sounds like a joke, and in fact more than a few, including the poet Robert Service, have poked fun at the concept. But ice worms are real. Alaska's glaciers are literally crawling with them.

A glacial geologist on one of John Muir's Alaska expeditions made the first scientific note of ice worms in 1887. At less than an inch long,

Portage Valley is among several places where the stealthy observer will find ice worms.
PHOTO BY B. B. MACKENZIE

the worms look like bits of black thread. Hundreds of thousands of them, millions even, appear on the surface of glacier ice in the evenings. They are very temperature sensitive, with thirty-two degrees Fahrenheit their ideal. At temperatures much above or below that, the worms appear to liquefy and disintegrate, so even holding one in the palm of your hand can put an end to it.

Ice worms have large mouths for feeding on red algae, and their heads are also big for their bodies, topped with a large pore that may secrete a substance that helps them burrow through the ice. During the day, they'll wriggle down to six feet below the surface.

A great place to learn more about ice worms is the Begich-Boggs Visitor Center at Portage Valley, where rangers occasionally lead "ice worm safaris." They suggest looking for ice worms in slushy snow and in puddles of glacial melt around the edge of a glacier, taking care to avoid areas of active calving. Walking on glaciers can be dangerous, so stick to the edges, and avoid the faces of glaciers that are known to calve. Use a shovel and spoon to poke around for the critters, and don't forget that your hand means instant death to these little guys.

Outhouse Exposure
Ptarmigan Creek

With plenty of backcountry that precludes plumbing, Alaska has more than its share of outhouses. They come in all shapes and sizes: one-holers and two-holers, fancy and plain, heated and rustic. One of the most unusual is a wall-less throne on a hill along the Ptarmigan Creek Trail, adding another dimension of meaning to the term "open air."

The Ptarmigan Creek Trail begins in the US Forest Service Ptarmigan Creek Campground at mile 23.2 of the Seward Highway. It follows a lovely creek to a conifer forest where, from the left side of the trail, signs point the way to the nicely constructed but utterly exposed privy. A partner to warn away other users offers your best chance at privacy.

Continue past the outhouse to the expansive and secluded Ptarmigan Lake, where the trail dead-ends 3.5 miles from its beginning.

The outhouse along the Ptarmigan Creek Trail
offers spectacular views . . . of you.
PHOTO BY G. M. FERENCY

★ ★

Alaska's Got Talent

Seward

Long before television shows featuring tap dancers and flame throwers, Alaska conducted its own talent search. The winner was thirteen-year-old Benny Benson, the boy from the orphanage who designed the Alaska state flag.

After his Aleut mother died when Benson was three, his Swedish fisherman father left Benson at the Jesse Lee Home for children in Unalaska, along the Aleutian chain. Swamped with children after the 1918 Spanish influenza epidemic decimated coastal villages, the Jesse Lee Home was relocated to Seward. It was there that Benson's seventh-grade teacher encouraged her students to draw flags for a contest commissioned by the territorial legislature in 1926.

Benson's winning design was simple: eight stars of gold, in the shape of the Big Dipper and its companion North Star, on a field of blue. "The North Star is for the future of the State of Alaska, the most northerly in the union," Benson explained in his entry. "The Big Dipper is for the Great Bear, symbolizing strength." The blue was reminiscent of the Alaskan sky and the state flower, the forget-me-not.

Years later, the composer of Alaska's state song would open it with the lyrics describing Benson's creation: "eight stars of gold on a field of blue," followed by a second verse that paid direct tribute to the young artist.

A shy boy, Benson was never completely comfortable with the fame and recognition he received. When visitors came to the Jesse Lee Home to see the boy who'd designed the flag, he'd sometimes take to the woods and hide till they left. Nevertheless, buildings were named for him, and the town of Seward now officially recognizes the Fourth of July as Benny Benson Day.

Four years after he led the 1959 Independence Day parade in Alaska's capital city of Juneau to celebrate Alaska's admission as a state, Benson donated the watch he received as a prize in the contest to the

At the Jesse Lee Home, Benny Benson holds the
flag he designed at age thirteen.
ALASKA STATE LIBRARY, BENSON BENNY ASL-P01-1921

★ ★

Alaska State Museum. After its main building sustained heavy damage in Alaska's 1964 Good Friday earthquake, the Jesse Lee Home was abandoned, but the remaining structures still stand at 1824 Phoenix Road in Seward.

Run up the Mountain—and Back
Seward

It's the Fourth of July, and if you're waiting for fireworks, you'll be disappointed—Alaska's long summer daylight keeps us from the displays that draw oohs and ahs in the Lower 48 states. Ever innovative, Alaskans came up with their own Independence Day entertainment, in the form of watching runners make a grueling assent up Mount Marathon and back.

Treacherous cliffs. Fields of loose scree. Waterfalls. A mile and a half up the mountain, and a mile and a half down again. The grueling footrace attracts runners from all over the globe.

According to legend, the annual tradition got started as two Alaskan sourdoughs considered from their seats at the bar whether it was possible to run to the top of the mountain and back in less than an hour. The first race, held in 1915, proved that wager was off by only a hair—the actual time up and back was two minutes more than an hour.

The race is amazingly popular. On the Fourth of July, the streets of Seward are lined with thousands of spectators all hoping to catch a glimpse of the runners who dare to sprint to the top of a mountain and back. A fee-based lottery is held to determine who can enter, beginning on January 1 of each year. Special competitions are held for children and seniors. The race course is hazardous, and entrants are urged to be prepared for everything from heat stroke to wet slippery rocks. One year the front-runner collapsed just prior to reaching the finish.

Finish times have now dipped well below that old sourdough wager. These days, top finishers typically arrive in under fifty minutes.

★ ★

Polar Bear Plunge

Seward

It's the third weekend in January. Dark. Snowy. Cold. Very cold. So what's an Alaskan to do? Go jump in the frigid waters of Resurrection Bay.

That's how the folks in Seward see it, anyhow. It was 1986 when the first hardy souls volunteered to dress in costume (insulated coveralls?) for a quick January swim. They rounded up sponsors who pledged money for charity if they'd really go through with it. The American Cancer Society embraced the chance to raise money for their cause, and the Polar Bear Plunge has since grown into an annual event that draws literally busloads of spectators from Anchorage to Seward to witness the madness. Holland America/Princess runs special Polar Bear Jump shuttles down the Seward Highway, and the Seward fire department and the Seward ambulance service are on hand to help shivering swimmers out of the water.

If you want to take the plunge, you have to get on board early. Registrations open in late summer, when you can still be fooled into thinking the water can't be *that* cold. All available slots are generally filled within a few weeks. Not surprisingly, this crazy event has drawn a lot of media interest, including television coverage in the Lower 48 and write-ups in *Reader's Digest* and *Outside* magazine. Live radio broadcasts of the foolhardy plunging have reached audiences as far away as Sydney, Australia.

If you're not up for a very cold bath, there's plenty of other fun to be had at what's now a full weekend festival in Seward. Of special interest: bowling with frozen turkeys outdoors at the American Legion, immediately following the plunge.

Sawfest
Soldotna

Some artists use a palette and brush. Some wield a pen. Some chisel fine details into rock. Then there are the guys with the chain saws.

In celebration of chain-saw art, the Town of the Living Trees gallery in Soldotna hosts Sawfest, an annual three-day competition among these modern-day, buzz-sawing wood carvers. It's a chance for the artists to take a break from their usual tourist fare and let whimsy and imagination run wild.

After three days and sometimes three nights of carving, with their ears ringing and their hands vibrating, the chain-saw artists submit their work to a panel of judges. First place in 2010 went to *Giddy-up* by Derrick Stanton of Nikiski. Stanton claims not to have ever picked up a chain saw before arriving in Alaska in 2003, but he managed to transform an eight-foot log into an elaborate carving of a cowboy being bucked by a salmon. The previous year, Stanton also took first with a carving of a boy surfing on a halibut.

Mine, Mine, Mine, a carving depicting an angler and a bear tussling over a salmon, was the 2010 second place winner. Third place went to *Sly Fish*, a painted piece depicting two red fox looking longingly at a bald eagle perched just out of reach, a salmon clutched in its talons.

The Town of the Living Trees, at 41672 Sterling Highway, was founded in part to encourage the use of beetle-killed spruce trees in artwork. Standing dead spruces contribute to fire danger on the Kenai Peninsula, and culling them helps thwart that danger. With a similar goal, Stanton has opened the Derrick Stanton Logworks and Gift Shop near Soldotna's Spur Lounge, where he invites visitors to watch him carve and, if they like, order a custom piece. What he and his fellow artists can do with a log and a chain saw isn't just curious—it's amazing.

★ ★

Wilderness Woman Contest and Bachelor Auction

Talkeetna

If you've been to Talkeetna, you understand why the Bachelor Society is the big social group there. In this quintessential Alaska backwoods town (the old TV show *Northern Exposure* is said to have been modeled on life in Talkeetna), things get a little slow in the winter, and it's not exactly a mecca for high-styling women. Never mind. Those aren't the sort of women the bachelors are wanting, as is evident from the requirements of the Wilderness Woman Contest.

Held each December, the tongue-in-cheek contest begins with a qualifier: hauling buckets of water from the creek. The five top finishers advance to round two, where contestants prepare sandwiches and serve beer to lounging bachelors (pouring the beer on their heads gets you disqualified) and then don snowshoes to stalk fake ptarmigan and snag fake salmon, all while steering clear of a renegade "moose."

Round three involves filling sleds with split wood and transporting it by snowmachine to feed the bonfire around which Talkeetna's eminently desirable bachelors swap their tall tales. It's all in good fun, with prizes to the top three finishers.

After the women have had their moment in the spotlight, the party reconvenes with a Bachelor Auction, where ladies who've not yet had their fill of bachelor shenanigans bid for a drink and a dance with their favorite single guys. Between them, the Wilderness Woman Contest and the Bachelor Auction are the social events of Talkeetna's year, especially now that the summer Moose Dropping Festival has been "dropped" due to some overly poopy behavior. Women and bachelors have been traveling from all over the state for over twenty-five years to take part in the winter event, and good money is raised to benefit charity.

If this bachelor-filled fun isn't enough to satisfy, there's also an Ole and Lena Ski Relay held on the same December Saturday. Required are one Ole and one Lena (or at least the costumes must fit); at the relay transition point, teams must tell Ole and Lena jokes—jokes that poke fun at a stereotypical Norwegian man and his wife—before they can move on.

Wal-Mike's

It's Alaska's answer to Wal-Mart: Wal-Mike's, a sprawling shop of odds, ends, curiosities, trash, and treasures at mile 115 of the Parks Highway in Trapper Creek.

In a state known for its lax zoning and its junk collectors, Wal-Mike's is one of the best-known examples of both. The yard and the store are jam-packed with collectibles and artifacts. With each item comes a story that owner Mike Carpenter will happily tell, though it's up to you to decide whether his tales are fiction or fact. Among his claims: The stuff he sells is all new; he just hasn't sold any of it for some time now.

Cameras and a sense of humor are encouraged for visits to what's billed as an "old-fashioned Alaskan store." And if you want to buy something, Mike won't stop you. He'll even let you hand feed his pet reindeer, Ivory and Two Socks.

If you're wondering, yes, we have Wal-Marts in Alaska. But Wal-Mike's is a whole lot more fun.

At the world-famous Wal-Mike's Alaskan shopping outlet, it's not all about sales.
PHOTO BY B. B. MACKENZIE

✳ ✳

Off Shaky Ground
Valdez

What to do when your town collapses in one of the biggest earth-quakes of the century? Yes, you rebuild, but in the case of the South-central community of Valdez, you do it on firmer ground. That's why the town of Valdez today lies three miles from where it once was.

On March 27, 1964, Valdez was leveled by a 9.2 earthquake origi-nating from an epicenter forty-five miles to the west. Many of Alaska's coastal communities took a beating, but Valdez, a port town dating back to the Klondike gold rush, was among the hardest hit. Massive sections of earth slid into the bay, wiping out two docks and destroy-ing streets, buildings, and homes.

On the waterfront, the Valdez tank farm after the damage by the 1964 earthquake but before it was destroyed by fire
UAF-1972-153-248, ARCHIVES, UNIVERSITY OF ALASKA FAIRBANKS

217

When it came time to rebuild Valdez, the Army Corps of Engineers worked to find a more stable spot. Three miles east of the old town site, they found it at the base of Mineral Creek, where gravel one hundred feet down meant another earthquake wouldn't collapse the town in on itself.

Sixty-two buildings that survived the 1964 quake were hauled from the old town site to the new location. Though it took four years to complete the town's transformation, for its resilience Valdez earned All-American City status in 1965. Today, all that remains of Old Valdez are dock pilings, the post office foundation, and a few gravel roads.

To commemorate that town that was lost, the Valdez Museum (www.valdezmuseum.org) created the Remembering Old Valdez exhibit at 436 South Hazelet Street, where a sprawling one-twentieth-scale replica meticulously reconstructs four hundred buildings and sixty city blocks as they were prior to the quake. By touring the replica while listening to audiotaped interviews with Old Valdez survivors, visitors can sample the sounds and stories of the town that had to be moved off shaky ground.

Cheers! Salmon's Not Just for Forks
Wasilla

Let those other towns have their microbrews. In Wasilla, they've got Smoked Salmon Vodka, a specialty beverage made at the local Alaska Distillery.

Alaska Distillery made its first big splash in the market with Alaska Permafrost Vodka, distilled from the Matanuska Valley's sweet and tasty thin-skinned potatoes. But potato vodka wasn't such a big novelty, so distiller Toby Foster decided to push the envelope by turning fish into booze.

Foster's not giving away his secret recipe—it took a lot of gagging to get through the first few attempts. But the process involves a lot of fish handling: skinning, deboning, defatting, and shredding smoked

Behind the bar at Sheep Mountain Lodge, mile 113.5 Glenn Highway, Smoked Salmon Vodka and Blueberry Vodka, both manufactured by the Alaska Distillery in Wasilla
PHOTO BY G. M. FERENCY

salmon, which then gets a bath in a vat of ethanol to impart its flavor, which is more smoky than fishy.

What to do with Smoked Salmon Vodka? If you're not keen on trying it straight up, you might mix it up in a Bloody Mary, which is the way some local bars serve it. Among those with this specialty beverage in their inventory is the Bear Tooth Grill bar (1230 West Twenty-Seventh Avenue, Anchorage; 907-276-4200; www.beartooththeatre.net).

Secret City
Whittier

A quick look at a map shows why Alaska held such strategic importance for the United States during World War II. With fronts in the Pacific and Asia, not to mention air exchanges in a Lend-Lease program with Russia, the territory was a logistical necessity and also a potential target. One strategic requirement: an ice-free port, accessible by railroad, to get supplies in and out of Alaska while the highway through Canada from the mainland United States was under construction. Ideally, the port would be a secret from enemy forces.

That's how the town of Whittier came to be. A short ride by rail from Anchorage, it not only offered the required ice-free port, but it was also blessed by bad weather for a good part of the winter—low ceilings that hid the army's activities from enemy aircraft.

For a long time, the town consisted of only two residential/office complexes: the Buckner Building and what's now known as the Begich Building, named after Alaska senator Nick Begich, who was killed in 1972 when his plane crashed in Prince William Sound not far from Whittier.

Before the army pulled out in 1960, the town's population had grown to 1,200, but it has since fallen to 175 hardy Whittierites. With the Buckner Building condemned, they all hunker down in the condo units of Begich Towers—there's virtually no private land in the town, which is more or less owned by the railroad. The Begich Towers themselves are like a small city: Inside there's a beauty shop, bakery, tanning salon, convenience store, post office, and church. An underground tunnel leads to the school, which typically serves thirty to forty students in kindergarten through grade twelve.

The tunnel is handy in winter, when Whittier gets socked in by an average of twenty feet of snow. But when it's not raining, the summers are glorious. Water shimmers in Whittier's new harbor and in the nearby cruise ship docks, where tourists unload literally by the boatloads.

★ ★

Getting to Alaska's hidden city is a lot easier now than it once was. Previously there was only one set of tracks tunneling through the mountains to Whittier. Everyone and everything had to be moved in and out by either railroad or boat. But in 2000, the railroad opened the tunnel to single-lane vehicle traffic in a schedule that works around both trains and vehicles headed the opposite direction. Getting to Alaska's secret town requires some advance planning, but when the sun's shining and the fish are in, it's well worth the trip.

Begich Towers in Whittier
PHOTO BY G. M. FERENCY

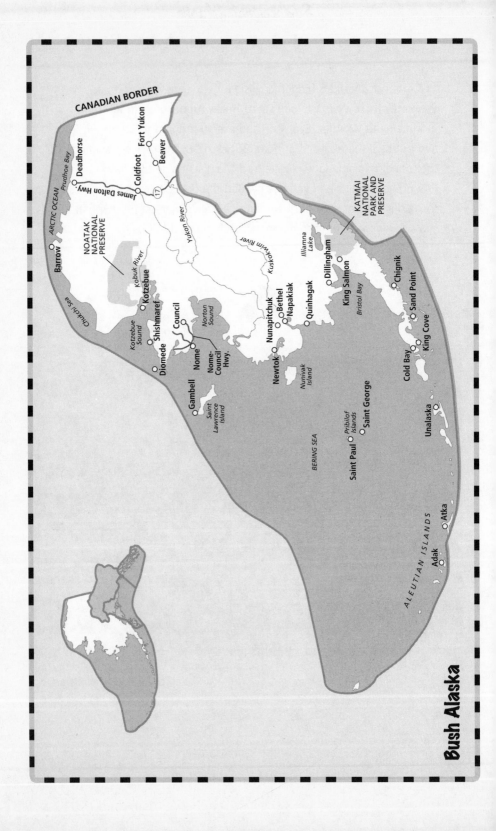

Bush Alaska

4

Bush Alaska

Alaska is the *only state in the Union with its own "bush." Bush Alaska refers to those parts of the state that are difficult to access, remote places that can be reached only by bush planes flown by bush pilots. Geographically, most the state is in the Bush, though most of the population lives on the road system or in one of the off-road towns that aren't small enough or remote enough to be considered part of the Bush.*

When you're in Bush Alaska, it's easy to feel like you're in another country, and in some places, even another era. Land in a village, and you may not hear English but Yup'ik or Inupiaq or Athabascan. You're more likely to get around by snowmachine or all-terrain vehicle or small boat than by car. There will likely be one school serving students in kindergarten through grade twelve. There won't be a hospital, but there will perhaps be a clinic manned by a village health aide. There won't be a police force, but there may be a Village Public Safety Officer. There may or may not be running water. Electricity will likely come from a bank of diesel generators. Village populations run from a few dozen to a few hundred people.

When Alaskans consider the Bush, they think in terms of four major areas: the Aleutians, Southwest Alaska, Northwest Alaska, and Northern Alaska. Each of these regions encompasses a land mass similar to one of the Lower 48 states. Just the Lower Kuskokwim Delta portion

★ ★

of Southwest Alaska, for instance, is as big as the state of Oregon. Each region is served by a hub city or two: in the Aleutians, it's Dutch Harbor and its sister city of Unalaska; in Southwest, it's Bethel; in Northwest, it's Nome and Kotzebue ("Kotz"); in Northern Alaska, it's Barrow. Interior Alaska has some Bush villages, too; for these, Fairbanks is the hub.

The Aleutian Islands are the traditional home of the Alutiiq people, who were enslaved by the Russians in the eighteenth century and who were relocated to internment camps by the US government when Attu and Kiska were attacked during World War II. Today, most people recognize Dutch Harbor, the rough, stormy launching point for the fishing fleets featured in the Deadliest Catch reality television show. Rainy and windy, the Aleutians are also haunting in beauty and remarkably remote. Ferry service from one end of the chain to the other takes several days, and flying to the Pribilof Islands beyond the end of the chain takes roughly four hours from Anchorage. Here, where cargo is precious and prices are high, traditions like the annual Aleutian Pumpkin Run mean a lot.

Traditional home to the Yup'it, Southwest Alaska was the last part of the state, and of the country, where Outside influences clashed with native traditions. In country potholed by thousands of permafrost lakes, lacking the vast quantities of furs, whales, and minerals that attracted strangers to other parts of the Bush, the Yup'it maintained their remarkably adaptive lifestyle with relatively little interference for decades longer than was possible in other parts of Alaska. Here the culture is strong and the traditional language intact. Outdoor steam baths, honey buckets (indoor substitutes for outhouses), legends of the Hairy Man and the Little People and the Iliamna Lake monster—these may seem curious to outsiders, but they're part of life in Southwest Alaska.

Bush Alaska

★ ★

Whalers and prospectors flooded Northwest Alaska in the nineteenth century. The last and most remote of the big northern gold rushes happened in Nome at the turn of the century. A huge tent city stretched over miles of Nome's beach, where even the sands were believed to be made of gold. Here there were roads, but they went only from Nome to the gold fields, where they dead-ended. Aside from the vestiges left when the boom went bust—the train that rusts on the tundra, the smiling ivory Billikens carved by Inupiat carvers to bring miners good luck—the country of Northwest Alaska has produced its own notables, including the Kobuk Sand Dunes; the single tree of Kotzebue's "national forest"; and rocky King Island, its Inupiat village now deserted.

In the North, there were whales and, decades later, liquid gold, in the form of North Slope crude, which made the regional native corporation one of the most prosperous in the state. Northern Alaska is the only Bush region with a road running to it, and that's only to the oil fields. The rest of this vast frozen wilderness, including the farthest north city of Barrow with its farthest north high school football team and its farthest north Mexican restaurant, can only be reached by air.

Bush Alaska is a fascinating place. Most Alaskans never get out there—it's too remote and expensive. But for those of us who are lucky enough to visit, or perhaps to live there, it's a place you'll never forget. Remote. Isolated. And so unique you'll hardly know how to describe it.

Rat Islands
Aleutians

No humans live there, and they're not a place you'd have wanted to visit: a cluster of islands overrun with rats. But it's all better now.

Brown rats aren't native to Alaska, but in the eighteenth century a Japanese ship wrecked near these islands in the Aleutian chain, which are closer to Japan than to Anchorage. Rats streamed from the wreckage. Subsisting on the eggs of migrating birds, the rats didn't take long to take over since there were no predators to keep their population in check. Landing there in 1827, Russian captain Fyodor Litke was quick to name them the Rat Islands.

While nearby islands spared from the invasion of rats were noisy with the sounds of nesting birds, the Rat Islands became strangely silent, exhibiting a problem that plagues islands worldwide: Once rats invade, they thrive at the expense of native wildlife. On these particular islands, the rats subsisted mainly on the eggs and chicks of nesting waterfowl. So the US Fish and Wildlife Service began a plan to eradicate the rats in hopes that waterfowl populations would rebound.

Thanks to some tasty pellets infused with a poison that killed rats but harmed nothing else, these islands are now due for a name change. For the first time in over two centuries, the Rat Islands are free of rats. Birders love the remote Aleutians for the large variety of migratory waterfowl that can be seen there, and now the Rat Islands will be no exception.

Blanket Toss
Barrow

Blankets aren't just for sleeping—at least not in Barrow and other communities along Alaska's North Slope. As part of the traditional Inupiat whaling festival Nalukataq, the whale harvest is celebrated each year in June with a huge sealskin or walrus-skin blanket that is flung like a trampoline, held down not by poles or springs but by the willing hands of neighbors and friends.

The blanket toss with seal skins and bunny boots
PHOTO BY G. M. FERENCY

★ ★

The summer festival is a time for offering thanks for nature's bounty and for distributing whale meat preserved from the hunt. Prayers are made, speeches given, and then the fun begins. Originally the whaling captains and their wives were first to be "tossed" on the big skin blanket. As they were propelled in the air, they would throw gifts at the crowd to symbolize the community spirit of provision and giving. Today, candy is thrown.

The traditional blanket is sewn from the skins of bearded seals and stretched between four beams at waist height. Villagers flip the blanket at the edges to send the whalers soaring. With participants dressed in traditional *qaspeqs* (women's clothing) and sometimes in parkas and mukluks, the blanket toss is a colorful event that can last several hours before the celebration turns to a feast, complete with traditional Inupiat dancing.

If you can't get to Barrow, you can check out the blanket toss during the Anchorage Fur Rondy festival (see page 174) each February. Near the carnival rides at Third Avenue and E Street, a traditional sewn-skin blanket with handles is manned by volunteers who'll let you try the human-held trampoline for free. In exchange for your time in the air, be sure to take a turn holding the blanket. A tightly-held blanket is essential for a good toss, and you'll get a great upper-body workout along with a sense of community spirit, which is what the blanket toss is all about.

Farthest North Football
Barrow

It's only a stone's throw from the Arctic Ocean. Polar bears may wander nearby. Snow will likely fall before the season begins. Football is a hardy sport, and it doesn't get much hardier than in Barrow, Alaska, where the country's farthest north football team runs its plays.

A whaling community of 4,500 along the Bering Sea coast, Barrow is not exactly a prime spot for the gridiron. Underlain with permafrost, there are no roads leading to Barrow from anywhere else, which means the town's athletic teams have to travel hundreds of miles by jet to compete with other state schools, and all supplies have to be shipped in by air.

In many ways, Barrow is a place trapped in time. While some residents still engage in traditional activities like whaling and hunting, the influx of the Internet and television, combined with alcohol and drug problems, have left many young people at odds with themselves and their traditions.

Not everyone in the community saw football as the best way to engage young people. But as rookies were recruited to play, to officiate, and to coach, parents began seeing their boys come together with a sense of school pride and community. Some even compared it to whaling, with its reliance on the harpooner's perfect throw and the importance of teamwork.

In its first year, Barrow's team played on a gravel field not far from the Arctic Ocean. Then a Florida football mom heard about their enthusiasm and raised funds for Project Alaska Turf. Thanks to the generosity of donors and shipping companies, the Barrow Whalers now play on a bright blue field of artificial turf. There's no word yet on whether the blue is any sort of deterrent to polar bears.

Farthest North Mexican Restaurant
Barrow

Looking for a taco on the tundra? Disregard the fact that on Alaska's northern coast, you're over three thousand miles from Mexico. Pepe's North of the Border will feed all your Mexican food cravings.

Pepe's is one of the best-known restaurants in Alaska, and it's not only because of the big distance it bridges. Its longtime owner, Fran Tate, is a well-known community figure in Barrow. She started Pepe's in a two-bedroom house and grew it into a popular eatery that seats over two hundred taco crunchers.

In the far-north community of Barrow, population 4,500, Tate has had a big impact beyond tacos and enchiladas. She ran much-needed

★ ★

water delivery and sewage disposal businesses when both what went into a house and came out of it had to be delivered by truck. She also was one of the longtime volunteers at Barrow's public radio stations.

Oddly, Tate never considered herself much of a cook. Pepe's is staffed by loyal employees who cater to tourists in the summer and to hungry townsfolk in the winter. The restaurant has received national attention, including a feature in *Time* magazine and a reported encounter involving entertainer Johnny Carson and an *oosik* bone.

Tate hasn't let fame go to her head. When the Barrow Whaler football team won its season opener in 2010, she served up burgers to the hungry athletes. In the end, Pepe's is a great hometown restaurant, where hearts are warm no matter how cold it gets outside.

Unfrozen Ice Cream

Alaska has one of the highest per capita rates of ice-cream consumption in the country, which is a little surprising for someplace so cold. But if you're not inclined to eat a frozen dessert in a frozen place, Bush Alaska offers an alternative: Eskimo ice cream or, by its more proper Yup'ik name, *akutaq*.

Especially popular in Southwest Alaska, *akutaq* is made with three basic ingredients: shortening, sugar, and berries. The shortening and sugar are worked by hand to a smooth, whipped consistency, and then the berries are stirred in. Other common additions are fish, seal oil, and instant mashed potatoes.

Once you get past the cholesterol hang-up of a dessert that is nearly all fat, *akutaq* is a delicious treat. A staple at potlatches and other feasts, it's also great for warming up when you're cold, and it takes up no space in the freezer.

Japanese Moses

Beaver

During World War II, Japan attacked the Alaskan islands of Attu and Kiska on the Aleutian chain. But decades earlier, a friendly Japanese one-man "invasion" by Kyosuke "Frank" Yasuda led to the founding of Beaver, a remote village on the Yukon River.

Born in 1868 to a wealthy family in Japan's Miyagi prefecture, Yasuda's parents died when he was fifteen years old, so Yasuda apprenticed himself to the Mitsubishi Shipping Company, which took him to California, where he later signed on as a cabin boy with the US Revenue Cutter *Bear*.

When the *Bear* got locked in the ice near Barrow one winter, Yasuda left the ship and took employment with Charlie Brower. When the cutter left in the spring, Yasuda stayed on in Barrow, where he learned trading skills from Brower, who also encouraged him to learn the customs and language of the Native Inupiat.

Yasuda married Nevalo, daughter of an important Inupiat whaler, and together they began trading with people along the coastal rivers. Times in Barrow were hard, with commercial whaling pressure drastically reducing the resource upon which Inupiat culture depends. Starvation threatened, and though US relief ships brought foodstuffs to the regions, they were a poor substitute for the traditional diet. There was talk of the need to move inland, possibly to subsist on caribou as did the native people of Anaktuvik Pass.

In 1903, prospectors Thomas Carter and Samuel Marsh persuaded the Yasudas to guide them on an expedition up the Canning and Chandalar Rivers in search of gold. After much searching, Yasuda and Carter made a large strike at Little Squaw Creek, which Carter had named for the Yasudas' infant daughter. While berry picking in the area the following summer, Nevalo discovered the mother lode, the source of the creek deposits they'd been mining.

One of the last Alaskan gold rushes was to the Chandalar region in 1907. Yasuda insisted that Carter maintain the Inupiat interest in the

★ ★

**Facing the camera, "Japanese Moses" Frank Yasuda
on a hunting expedition**
UAF-1991-0045-6, ARCHIVES, UNIVERSITY OF ALASKA FAIRBANKS

claims, and in 1910, he set up a supply point along the Yukon River, which he called Beaver. On a visit to Barrow, the Yasudas found the community still suffering from the depletion of whales, and so they organized families to travel with them through the Brooks Range to Beaver. The trip took almost two years, earning Yasuda the nickname "Japanese Moses."

* *

The town of Beaver prospered. Three languages and cultures mingled there: Japanese, Inupiat, and Gwich'in, an Indian group from Alaska's Interior. Even today, Japanese, Gwich'in, and English are all taught at the school in Beaver. As many as three small planes daily bring visitors to see the town founded by the "Japanese Moses." Native guide Cliff Adams (www.beaverlodgetours.com) conducts tours of the village that begin with a forty-five-minute flight from Fairbanks over the Arctic Circle and include a stop at Yasuda's final resting place in Beaver.

Snow Legal
Bethel

In Bush Alaska, you can't get around in the usual ways. Most towns and villages aren't connected by roads, and in the western and northern parts of the state, much of the ground is soggy, unstable permafrost, which makes road building tough. Locals look forward to winter, when the frozen rivers are plowed and used as highways. From freeze-up to breakup, vehicles travel the Kuskokwim River and the smaller rivers and sloughs that feed into the Kuskokwim.

If trucks and taxis can use snow and ice for roads, why not let snowmachines (also called sno-gos; no self-respecting Alaskan says "snowmobile") ride the roadways? In 2007, that question was taken up by the city council of Bethel, a Kuskokwim River community of six thousand residents that serves as a hub for fifty-some villages. Given the high cost of gasoline that has to be brought in by barge, the council passed an ordinance allowing snowmachines and all-terrain vehicles to circumvent the usual requirements for street-legal vehicles.

The ordinance didn't start anything new. For decades, residents and visitors from neighboring villages had been cruising Bethel's streets by four-wheeler and snowmachine. The new law simply redefined what was "street legal." Now it's a lot closer to "anything goes," which is what you find on the streets of Bethel.

Little People

Spend any time in the predominantly Yup'ik region of Southwest Alaska and you'll likely hear about the little people, or *cingssiik*. These magical people reportedly appear from time to time on the tundra, bringing good luck or bad, depending on the circumstances.

Those who claim to have encountered the *cingssiik* say that time passes in an instant while in their presence. One traditional story tells of a hunter whose luck changed for the better after he grabbed a *cingssiik* that came out of the walls of a house. He held onto the little guy until the *cingssiik* granted him his wish to become lucky in hunting.

Another reports the mischief done by *cingssiik* that finished repairing fishing nets but left them inside out. There's also a tale of a man who happened upon a tiny foot-long sled. When he returned the next day, the sled was gone, and there were tiny tracks leading away from the place it had been.

In 2008, the *Anchorage Daily News* ran a report from Marshall, a Yukon River village, about a young Yup'ik boy who mysteriously disappeared from his home. He was found dazed but unharmed in the middle of the tundra, with no tracks leading toward or away from him. When quizzed by the snowmachiner who found him, he said he had been brought into an area rumored to be inhabited by *ircenrraat*, the little people who purportedly live near the mountains. While with the *ircenrraat*, he said he spoke with a girl who had been kidnapped by the little people decades before.

In northern Alaska, the little people are known as *imminauruks* or *enukins*. They are described as elf-like creatures with superhuman strength and speed. According to some, these people who stand three to four feet in height separated long ago from other Inupiat. Today they're purported to live in underground caves and dress in caribou skins, appearing every so often to lend a hand or to play tricks.

★ ★

The Town That Wouldn't Die

Coldfoot

At mile 175 of the Dalton Highway between Fairbanks and Prudhoe Bay, there's a well-trafficked truck stop—in fact, it's pretty much the only stop on the highway that runs north to the oil fields—built partly by the truckers themselves.

The trucker-constructed stop is at Coldfoot, which from 1898 to 1912 was a booming gold mining community with two roadhouses, seven saloons, a gambling hall, and several "ladies" for whom surrounding creeks were named. But better prospects were found at nearby Wiseman, and many of the buildings from Coldfoot were either relocated or leveled for firewood.

But as it turned out, Coldfoot was a community that wouldn't say die. When the Trans Alaska Pipeline System was under construction in the 1970s, Coldfoot was a worker camp along the Dalton Highway, also called the Haul Road because it was built exclusively to haul materials to build facilities at Deadhorse on the North Slope. After the initial construction boom ended, Iditarod musher Dick Mackey, father of Lance Mackey (see page 96), dragged a school bus to Coldfoot where he sold hamburgers to truckers on their way to Deadhorse.

Looking for more than a school bus for their road breaks, the truck drivers dropped empty packing crates from the materials they'd been hauling, and they even took up hammers to pound together some walls of what is now the Coldfoot Cafe. On a pole raised in the center of the restaurant, the truckers engraved their names.

Initially considered a private road too dangerous for the public to travel, the Dalton Highway eventually was opened to private vehicles, and Coldfoot became a popular destination for tours taking visitors above the Arctic Circle. In addition to the cafe, there's now lodging, fuel, a gift shop, laundry, showers, and a post office at the town that wouldn't die.

Sphinx of Ophir
Council

Though known for its mountains, much of Alaska was flattened by glaciers during a series of Ice Age events. Now vegetated as tundra and forest, in these areas there's an occasional reminder of the big ice

The Sphinx of Ophir, an unusual rock formation near an abandoned mining town
FRANK AND FRANCES CARPENTER COLLECTION, LIBRARY OF CONGRESS

★ ★

that passed through, in the form of large rocks left behind. Among these ice-age remnants is the Sphinx of Ophir near the abandoned mining town of Council on the Seward Peninsula.

The Town That Isn't

Deadhorse

We're pretty sure there has never been a horse there, dead or alive. And though you might find a couple thousand people milling around there on any given day, the 2000 US census shows its population as five—and those five likely aren't supposed to claim it as their residence. That's because Deadhorse is the quintessential company town, an oil camp at the end of the Dalton Highway, also known as the Haul Road.

Deadhorse exists solely to serve the companies that transport crude oil through the Trans Alaska Pipeline System that begins there, at the Prudhoe Bay oilfield. Prudhoe Bay was named by a British explorer after one of his classmates, but no one seems quite sure where the name Deadhorse originated.

Thanks to the popular television show *Ice Road Truckers,* viewers have seen flat-screen images of Deadhorse: steel buildings elevated from the permanently frozen soils, an airport to accommodate crews flying in and out on weekly or biweekly shifts, and at the very end of the road, the Arctic Ocean.

Not so evident from the trucker show is the Deadhorse lifestyle. Because it's a company camp, alcohol is forbidden. In the dormitories, personnel typically "hot bunk," swapping with roommates on alternate shifts. Work weeks run sixty or eighty hours, with hefty overtime checks to compensate for the restrictive lifestyle.

At Deadhorse, there are no churches, no bars, no private residences or noncompany vehicles. There's only one store. During migration season, caribou browse the tundra near work camps, and an occasional polar bear wanders nearby. Far above the Arctic Circle, the sun stays up for over eighty days straight in the summer, and stays set for a simliar length of time in the winter.

★ ★

Village Voices
Fort Yukon

It's one thing to visit Alaska and marvel at how remote it seems from the Lower 48 states. It's another to venture into Alaska's truly remote places, villages well off the road system, communities only accessible by air or by water, with a steep price tag attached either way.

The Fort Yukon airstrip in 1961
UAA-HMC-0752-3-61A301: CHARLOTTE E. MAUK SLIDES, ARCHIVES AND
SPECIAL COLLECTIONS, CONSORTIUM LIBRARY, UNIVERSITY OF ALASKA ANCHORAGE

★ ★

Aside from the daunting transportation challenges, visitors lack easy access to most of Alaska's native villages. There are few if any hotels or other services for guests. But for over twenty years, Richard Carroll of Alaska Yukon Tours (907-662-2727) has offered tours of Fort Yukon. Guests travel by bush plane 145 miles from Fairbanks to Fort Yukon, where Carroll or one of his many relatives—the children in his parents' families number over a dozen on each side—bundle them into a vehicle to show them what it's like to live in a Alaska native village.

A stop at the local store reveals how much ordinary goods cost when they have to be brought in either by river barge or by plane. Without federal subsidies for mail and cargo service, the villages likely wouldn't survive. Heat is by fuel oil, which isn't cheap either. Running water isn't taken for granted. In lieu of a hospital there's a public health clinic, and instead of a police force, a Village Public Safety Officer (VPSO) maintains order. The school doubles as the community center, with the gym being a popular spot to shoot hoops.

There's a lot of history in Fort Yukon, which in addition to its role as a traditional Athabascan village was also a Hudson Bay trading post. Episcopalian missionary Howard Stuck, who led the first genuine successful expedition to the top of Mount McKinley, is buried here. Almost everyone in the village is related somehow to everyone else, and a lot of the locals are also related to the residents of Old Crow, Yukon Territory, which many visit by boat every summer.

It's not only Carroll's village tour that makes Fort Yukon unusually accessible to outsiders. Two recent books also tell of the way of life there: *Raising Ourselves* by Velma Wallis and *Eagle Blue: A Team, a Tribe, and a High School Basketball Season in Arctic Alaska* by Michael D'Orso.

Pipeline Pigs

Pigs have a reputation for wallowing in mud and muck, so it makes sense to use one to wade through the thick oil that travels the Alaska pipeline. We're not talking the oinking variety of pig, of course, but mechanical pigs that do the dirty work of cleaning inside the 850-mile pipeline that carries oil from the Prudhoe Bay fields to the port in Valdez.

Opened in 1974, the Trans Alaska Pipeline System represents a huge feat of engineering. Hundreds of animal crossings above and below ground, dozens of bridges, cooling tubes to keep the permafrost from melting, earthquake suspension systems—all are part of this modern-day marvel that snakes across Alaska. Also required is surveillance, and since engineers can't climb inside, they send the next best thing—mechanical "pigs" that are also charged with cleaning detail.

Technically, there's more than one type of pig that scrambles through our pipeline. Scraper pigs are engineered with bumper noses and lightweight materials to clean the pipeline so the oil flows freely at a rate that varies between five and seven miles per hour. Corrosion pigs are equipped with devices to measure pitting in the pipe walls, and deformation pigs are designed to sniff out dents and bends in the pipe.

Old Blubber

Gambell

While digging on Saint Lawrence Island for ivory to carve, Gambell resident Douglas Henry found some old blubber—very old, as it turns out. He had stumbled onto an ancient cache, a hole dug in permafrost to keep foods chilled or frozen.

After days of chipping away at the six feet of ice encasing the blubber, he delivered it to a wildlife biologist who was doing whale research on the islands. Due to its caching, the specimen was in fine condition, with part of the whale skin still attached. Analysis dated the *mangtak* at one thousand years old. The blubber apparently came from a bowhead whale, a species that is now protected, though subsistence use is allowed for the Siberian Yup'ik and Inupiat who depend on *mangtak* as a food source.

By studying the ancient blubber, scientists were able to determine that bowheads today are genetically quite similar to their ancestors. Their diet also appears similar, and it was noted that the whale skin contained levels of mercury equivalent to what are found in modern bowhead whales, suggesting that the contaminant comes not only from industrial sources.

Iliamna Lake Monster

Iliamna

Not far from the fishing town of Dillingham in the southwest corner of Alaska lies a huge, fish-filled, clear-water lake. Eighty miles long and over one thousand feet deep, it's no wonder Iliamna has spawned tales of a giant monster.

Like Nessie in Scotland's Loch Ness, the Iliamna Lake monster is rarely seen but much discussed. With a large head and slender body, the creature is reportedly ten feet long. There are stories of the creature thrashing the water so violently that boaters were afraid to go out. Some local residents even refuse to paint their boat bottoms red because there are rumors that red provokes rage in the monster.

★ ★

Pilots claim to have seen evidence of the Iliamna Lake monster from the air, though there haven't been any photos to back up these sightings. According to one tale reported in *Alaska* magazine, a pilot once spotted a school of four of the monsters swimming together, as if they were oversize sharks.

It's purportedly bad luck to spot the beast, which might explain the drop in recent reported sightings. Still, the Department of Fish and Game maintains an open file on the creature. There are all sorts of theories of what it might be: a beluga whale somehow adapted to freshwater, an octopus, a big lingcod, or a giant sturgeon (though no sturgeon have ever been caught in the lake). In a place as big as Lake Iliamna, in a place as big as Alaska, you're bound to run into a mystery or two, and our own Nessie seems determined to keep it that way.

Freshwater Seals

If you think seals only live in saltwater, you haven't been to Lake Iliamna, home to one of the few freshwater populations of seals in the world.

One of the largest lakes in Alaska, Iliamna is eighty miles long and twenty-two miles wide in places. Little is known about the population of freshwater seals that lives in the lake. They're commonly spotted in the summer, and while it was thought that they followed the Kvichak River to Bristol Bay in the fall, it appears that at least some overwinter at the frozen lake.

★ ★

Valley of Ten Thousand Smokes

Katmai

It was the geological event of the century, blackening skies and changing weather around the world. For fifteen years after the 1912 Novarupta blast, the Aleutian island of Katmai steamed with fumaroles,
earning the name "Valley of Ten Thousand Smokes" and attracting
scientists to study what the volcano left behind after it blew.

The two-day eruption in 1912 caused the collapse of the summit of Mount Katmai and the formation of a lava dome now called

**Without trees for fuel, scientists with the National
Geographic Expedition to the Valley of Ten Thousand
Smokes heated meals over the steaming fumeroles.**
UAA-HMC-0186-VOLUME3-1622: NATIONAL GEOGRAPHIC SOCIETY
KATMAI EXPEDITIONS PHOTOGRAPHS, ARCHIVES AND SPECIAL COLLECTIONS,
CONSORTIUM LIBRARY, UNIVERSITY OF ALASKA ANCHORAGE

★ ★

Novarupta. The explosion was heard as far away as Juneau, and ash fell as far south as Seattle. Spread across forty square miles, the Valley of Ten Thousand Smokes was formed of Novarupta ash deposits up to seven hundred feet deep, a geological phenomenon so spectacular and unique that in 1918 it was declared Katmai National Monument, transformed later to Katmai National Park and Preserve.

Visitors who fly to Katmai today can ride by bus to the Valley of Ten Thousand Smokes. The park encompasses fifteen active volcanoes built from the Pacific Ring of Fire, where tectonic plates collide beneath the ocean. Steam still plumes from time to time out of the park's Mount Trident as well as from Mount Mageik and Mount Martin. Through tuff, a type of rock formed of sand and volcanic ash, streams have cut dramatic gorges on the island, adding to a unique and haunting landscape.

Katmai National Park and the Valley of Ten Thousand Smokes can only be accessed by water or air. Most visitors fly by commercial jet from Anchorage 290 miles west to King Salmon, where they typically charter by air to Brooks Camp, where limited services are offered by the park concessionaire.

Stilted
King Island

In the days when cameras were new, it was one of the most photographed islands in Alaska. Today it's uninhabited, a rocky outpost in the Bering Sea, forty miles west of Cape Douglas.

Steep and without soil, the island's cliffs offered the only site for King Island's now-abandoned Inupiat village. Built entirely on stilts, the village attracted the attention of passengers steaming north during the Nome gold rush of 1900.

Captain James Cook named the island in 1778 during his Bering Sea expedition. Only a mile wide, the island was once the winter home of two hundred Inupiat living a subsistence lifestyle by harvesting sea mammals and fish. When the federal government closed the Bureau of Indian Affairs school on the island, everyone eventually moved to

**Houses on stilts attracted the attention of
seagoing passengers steaming past King Island
in the late nineteenth century.**
LOMEN BROTHERS, NOME, LIBRARY OF CONGRESS

the mainland. They still identify themselves as King Islanders, though,
and in recent years some have begun returning in the summer to visit.
The island and its residents are celebrated in the children's book *King
Island Christmas* by Jean Rogers and illustrated by Rie Muñoz, which
has been made into a musical.

Stonehenge Meets Alaska

Like ancient stones towering over the landscape, the remnants of Alaska's once state-of-the-art White Alice Communications System add an aura of mystery to our remote rural landscapes.

During the Cold War, the US military recognized the need for improved communications in Alaska, where many rural communities lacked even basic telephone service. To serve "control and warning" sites scattered throughout the state, the Air Force contracted with Western Electric to design and build a communications network called, for reasons unknown, White Alice.

Today the concave rectangular antennas—technically "tropospheric scatter antennas"—look more like ancient ruins than modern radar devices, but in their heyday the White Alice systems, ranging from 60 to 120 feet tall, were ultramodern. By scattering radio signals against the troposphere, White Alice was a huge improvement over old line-of-sight technologies. However, the systems were also expensive to build and maintain. In some locations airstrips had to be built for supplies to be delivered, fuel had to be stored to power the systems, and housing had to be arranged for technicians who monitored the White Alice operations.

The White Alice lifespan proved short. Within twenty years, satellite technology rendered the systems obsolete. One by one, the stations have been dismantled, sometimes at a cost greater than their original construction, owing to the presence of hazardous materials at the sites.

Of the original thirty-one White Alice stations, only a few of the "old girls" still stand, and none have seen use for decades. Among the survivors is a hilltop White Alice outside of Nome, where the old billboard antennas stand guard over the Bering Sea coast like sentinels. Residents joke that the White Alice is the town's drive-in theater. If you want to see one, you'd better act fast—no one knows how long it will be before the last one is torn down.

The White Alice site overlooking Nome
PHOTO BY B. B. MACKENZIE

★ ★

Survival Suit Race
Kodiak

Survival suits are serious business in Alaska, where the temperature of
ocean water sometimes dips below freezing. Hypothermia happens in
minutes, not hours, if someone is unlucky enough to fall overboard.
But sometimes a serious subject benefits from an injection of fun, as in
the Survival Suit Race during the annual Kodiak Crab Festival.

Over Memorial Day Weekend each spring, competitors in the Survival Suit Race must dash down a ramp, unpack and climb into a survival suit, swim one hundred yards in chilly ocean water, and board a
life raft. They work in teams of four, helping one another into the rafts
as they would in the event of a real maritime mishap. The big orange
suits are bulky and a little tough to maneuver, but they are genuine
lifesavers.

The town turns out to cheer on the contestants, and everyone gets
a good lesson in cold-water safety. Part of a crab festival that began
in 1958, the contest was started by the Kodiak Fisherman's Wives
and Associates before the era when survival suits became mandatory
on cold-water fishing vessels. They hoped the competition would get
fishermen familiar with gearing up in the suits and swimming with
them on. Though Kodiak's crab fishery was shut down in 1982 due to
a sharp decline in the resource, the Survival Suit Race continues as a
reminder of the importance of safety at sea.

Kobuk Sand Dunes
Kotzebue

Twenty thousand acres of sand. Temperatures that soar past one hundred degrees Fahrenheit. It sounds more like Africa than Alaska, but
these are the Kobuk Sand Dunes, a short charter flight from Kotzebue.

Part of the Kobuk Valley National Park, the dunes date back to the
Ice Age, when Northwest Alaska experienced not one but five major
glacial events. Strong easterly winds between two of the glaciations

★ ★

pushed large quantities of sand across approximately two hundred thousand acres (twenty-five square miles) of the Kobuk Valley. Tundra and taiga forest grew in over much of the sand, but three active areas of dunes remain: the Great Kobuk Sand Dunes, the Little Kobuk Sand Dunes, and the Hunt River Dunes. All offer a barren and silent testimony to the power of long-ago ice.

Some of the Great Kobuk Dunes reach over one hundred feet high, and together they make up the largest active field of sand dunes on the North American continent. Unlike the popular and heavily recreated dune fields along the Oregon coast, the Kobuk Dunes are wonderfully remote. To get there, grab a scheduled flight from Anchorage or Fairbanks to Kotzebue, a town of approximately four thousand, and then charter a plane to the active dunes area.

I Can See Russia
Little Diomede Island

During the 2008 presidential campaign, it was a favorite joke among late-night comedians: the claim of Alaska's governor, then a vice-presidential candidate, that our state's proximity to Russia gave her all the foreign policy experience a national leader would need.

While Russia is a long way from the Palin compound in Wasilla, there is a handful of Alaskan places from which, on a clear day, you really can see Russia from your house. The best example is Little Diomede Island, a rocky outpost in the middle of the Bering Sea separated from its neighbor, Big Diomede, by the Russian-American border.

First visited by Danish explorer Vitus Bering in 1728, the Diomede islands were once both inhabited by the Chukchi people. Today, only a weather station remains on Big Diomede, while Little Diomede has a population of approximately 150 people who live in close concert with the sea.

Less than three miles in diameter, Little Diomede is two and a half miles from Big Diomede. Both islands are part of what was once the

★ ★

Bering Land Bridge, a corridor that allowed migrations from Asia to North America. Located on the only part of Little Diomede that does not consist of sheer rock cliffs that drop straight to the sea, the native village there is called simply Diomede, or Inalik.

Aside from being able to look from their shores and see Russia, the residents of Little Diomede have another unique boast: From their houses, they can see tomorrow. The Russian-American border in that spot also serves as the international date line.

Marrying Ways

From attire to zoning, things tend toward the casual in Alaska, and weddings are no exception. You don't need a minister or a justice of the peace to get hitched here. Alaska statute allows almost anyone to get a one-day or a seasonal permit to act as a marriage commissioner. The provision dates back to the days when it wasn't all that easy to find a legal representative in many parts of the state.

If you want to help a happy couple tie the knot, you need only contact the court nearest to where the wedding will be held, providing your name as commissioner, the names of the bride and the groom, and the intended location of the wedding. The marriage license is still up to the bride and groom.

Even if you fail to register as a commissioner, the law still allows for a couple's marriage to stand, though you could face fines and penalties for performing the ceremony without the proper authority.

★ ★

Last Shot Fired

Little Diomede Island

The Civil War ended on April 9, 1865, but the last shot was actually fired more than two months later near Alaska's Little Diomede Island.

Perhaps you've never heard of the Civil War battles fought in Alaskan waters. Because Northern cities depended on oil rendered from whaling operations in Alaska, the CSS *Shenandoah* was dispatched to capture Yankee whalers in the North Pacific. Cleverly designed with a smokestack that could be lowered and rigging that could be swapped to camouflage the ship, the *Shenandoah* sank or captured

The SHENANDOAH towing prisoners from three burning whaling vessels in Behring's Straits, June 25, 1865.

A rendering of the Confederate warship CSS *Shenandoah* towing prisoners from three burning whaling ships in the Bering Strait on April 25, 1865, sixteen days after the South's surrender
ALASKA STATE LIBRARY, ASL-P62-317

thirty-eight Northern boats, taking one thousand prisoners but causing no fatalities.

Though he was shown newspaper articles documenting the South's surrender at Appomattox, *Shenandoah* Capt. James Waddell presumed the fighting was to continue in his part of the world. After his final conquest in Arctic waters on June 28, 1865, Waddell set sail for San Francisco, where he planned to launch a surprise attack.

Intercepted off the coast of California, he learned he and his crew were to be hanged. In disguise mode, he managed to escape and sail all the way to London without detection. The British harbored the crew, refusing to turn them over to US authorities.

All was eventually forgiven. A hundred years later, a US destroyer used in the Vietnam War bore Waddell's name. The site of the last shot fired was almost forgotten as well, except by those who want to amaze their friends with Civil War trivia.

Kick the Honey Bucket
Napakiak

It's a celebration any village would love—an event commemorating the end of the honey bucket era, because honey buckets are an Alaskan curiosity most would be happy to do without.

In rural Alaska, at least five thousand homes are without running water. And due to permafrost, the fix isn't as simple as digging a pit for an outhouse. In lieu of flush toilets, most have had to make do with five-gallon buckets walled off in a corner—sometimes only with curtains. Pine-scented cleanser is added to alter the smell, and some lucky family member gets assigned the chore of dumping the thing in an open waste area—all in all not conducive to health and happiness.

One by one, villages are kicking the "honey bucket" habit with funding from government agencies and with innovative plumbing strategies implemented by companies like the Canadian Cowater group, which has brought running water to twenty villages so far.

Upon completion of their 2010 project in Napakiak, Cowater threw a Kick the Honey Bucket party that included relay races with mock honey buckets and traditional Eskimo games.

To plumb without going underground, sewage is pumped to insulated sheds from which it's collected in a tank truck and deposited without all the hand hauling and spillage that comes with a honey bucket. It's a big improvement in living conditions that otherwise seem more like those in a third world country.

Sinking Town
Newtok

Like Venice, Italy, the village of Newtok in Southwest Alaska is sinking. But Newtok is a lot smaller, and its situation is a lot more precarious, so plans are underway to move the whole town as soon as funding is secured.

Until the federal government required them to settle in villages so the communities could have schools and public health services, the Yup'ik people of Southwest Alaska were nomadic, moving among seasonal camps. Originally a winter camp, the town site of Newtok is between the Ninglick River and a slough to the north.

As the river has widened, the permafrost soils under Newtok have begun to melt, and the town has sunk below sea level; it is a virtual island between the two waterways. Newtok's problems are compounded by sanitation issues. Human waste dumped out of honey buckets seeps back into the groundwater.

Warned that the town soon may not be habitable, the three hundred or so residents of Newtok have secured a new site called Mertarvik on high ground nine miles away. The work of moving their sinking town is underway, beginning with the planning and construction of a dock at the new site so that building supplies can be shipped in.

It's likely that climate change has contributed to the sinking of Newtok, as it has to the erosion of Shishmaref, an Inupiaq village to the north. Located on a barrier island and built mostly on sand, Shishmaref suffers from changing storm patterns and shrinking sea ice, which provides a natural buffer for coastal villages. Like Newtok, Shishmaref is sinking below sea level. Sea walls have helped fight off some of the pounding waves, but some walls have already failed, and the town's six hundred residents fear their community will no longer be livable if the erosion continues.

Bering Sea Ice Golf
Nome

The old adage about wanting what you can't have explains why golf events pop up in the strangest parts of Alaska. Fairbanks boasts the farthest north golf course, where play is routine except that it lingers well into sunlit summer nights. True, they've had problems with fox who like to trot off with the balls, and there's the occasional moose to contend with, but the greens grow lush in the long hours of daylight, and the games tend toward the serious.

But why let little details like grass dictate your game? In Alaskan Bush spirit, golfers in Nome take to the Bering Sea ice every spring, constructing their own par-41 course out of coffee cans and Astroturf. Forgot your tee? Not to worry. A spent shotgun shell works.

Head to Nome in mid-March, about the time the Iditarod mushers pull in after their thousand-plus-mile trek, and you can play a few rounds in the Bering Sea Ice Golf Classic. Expect golfers in costume and sled dogs recruited to caddy. Sand traps and water? Those are for wimps. Hazards here include slippery ice (good luck chasing that ball) and putt-stopping slush.

Tee off from the sea wall—it's all in good fun, with proceeds benefiting local charities.

Man Your Tubs

Nome

Research has yet to examine the Alaskan obsession with races. We have the usual foot races, the sprints and the marathons. Beyond events featuring motorcycles and cars, we also race snowmachines. And of course winter bring races with skis, snowshoes, and dogs.

Then there are bathtubs.

An old-fashioned bathtub of unknown origins hangs above Nome's Board of Trade Bar at 211 Front Street in Nome.
PHOTO BY B. B. MACKENZIE

★ ★

Every year, bathtubs race along Front Street in Nome, a town with a long history of racing that goes back to the All-Alaska Sweepstakes, a sled-dog race that capitalized on the town's gambling spirit once the gold rush died down. Though it may appear frivolous, promoters contend that the bathtub race has a serious purpose: to prove that, despite accusations to the contrary, Nome's residents do indeed know how to use bathtubs.

Spam

What is it about Alaska and Spam? We're speaking, of course, of the canned and (semi) edible variety, not the junk that infiltrates your e-mail box.

Not so long ago, it was tough to get any sort of fresh meat and produce in Alaska's Bush communities. Even today, with subsidized mail plane routes allowing for delivery of fresh foods, prices are high. Aside from those meats one can acquire with a gun or a net—fresh fish, bear, moose, ptarmigan, and the like—those that come in a can are immensely practical, which is why our state is the second largest consumer of Spam. (Hawaii is first.)

Mr. Whitekeys (see page 161), an Alaska comedy icon, made a big deal out of Spam when he ran the Fly By Night Club in Spenard. He encouraged customers to send in photos of themselves with their cans of Spam not only from around Alaska but from exotic locales worldwide. The canned meat product (does anyone know what's in it, exactly?) was featured prominently in the Fly By Night shows.

The race also has serious rules. Each team consists of one bather and four guards. Each guard wears a broad-rimmed hat—we can only speculate on its purpose—and carries a bathing implement, such as a bath mat or brush. Water is mandatory, as are suds.

When the flag drops, the plug's pulled, and teams must race, human drawn, to the finish. Water balloons and squirt guns may be used to distract opponents. The first tub that crosses the finish with at least ten gallons of water still sloshing takes the prize.

One can't help but wonder whether this crazy event was dreamed up in the Board of Trade, Nome's oldest saloon, where a tub hangs over the bar. To see the race and the bar, head to Nome the first week in September.

Last Train to Nowhere
Nome

It's a forlorn sight: Three rusting locomotives stranded on the Alaskan tundra. No stations. No rails. No one to ride them. Most days, there's nothing but the sound of the wind.

These three engines are all that remains of an attempt to connect what was once the thriving gold rush community of Solomon with rich mining districts fifty miles inland. Small rail operations were common in mining districts like Nome and Fairbanks during the early twentieth century, when there was plenty of big gold rush dreams to fuel them, but the Solomon–Council City venture was the first attempt to lay standard tracks in Alaska.

The now-stranded locomotives once chugged over the elevated railways of New York before the Council City and Solomon River Railroad hauled them north and put them to work hauling prospectors and the goods that supplied them. The discovery of gold in the Solomon River brought two thousand fortune-seekers to Solomon, though most were fair-weather miners who left in the winter. Still, the town had seven saloons, four hotels, and three stores.

★ ★

**The Last Train to Nowhere, on the tundra between the ghost towns
of Solomon and Council, thirty-three miles southeast of Nome**
PHOTO BY B. B. MACKENZIE

The route from Solomon to Council, a town that swelled to fifteen thousand on the banks of the gold-rich Ophir Creek, was surveyed in 1902, and in 1903 the first ten miles of track were constructed. A terminal was built in Dickson, on the east bank of the Solomon River.

But in 1906, funds dried up, and construction of the rail line stopped twenty miles short of Council. In 1913, a huge storm wiped out most of the terminal and a good part of the tracks. The rail cars were left to rust, and by the mid-1900s the once-prosperous communities they'd been commissioned to serve had turned into ghost towns.

★ ★

Iditarod Invitational
Nome

Nearly everyone has heard of the Iditarod, arguably the world's most famous sled-dog race. Far tougher, judging by factors like completion time and sheer loneliness, is the Iditarod Invitational, the world's longest human-powered winter race.

Following the famous Iditarod Trail from Anchorage to Nome, the Invitational, also known as the Iditaride, begins at the end of February each year. Contestants may bike, ski, or travel solely on foot. The record finish of a little over seventeen days is approximately twice the record finish for the Iditarod doggies.

A lone cyclist on a short winter day heads across the snow-covered wilderness to Nome.
PHOTO BY KATHARINA MERCHANT, ALASKA ULTRA SPORT

★ ★

There's no big cash prize or shiny Dodge truck awaiting the first racer to Nome as there is in the Iditarod Sled Dog Race, either. Contestants compete solely for the fun and the glory, though entry fees are waived the following year for first-place finishers hardy or crazy enough to tackle the 1,100-plus mile trek again. There's also a 350-mile version of the race from Anchorage to McGrath for those who prefer a "quick" trip.

Compared to the dog-driven Iditarod, this race is short on rules, and competitors seem to prefer it that way. There's no designated route you must follow, only checkpoints you must pass through. You must decide what to bring, and if you get into trouble in the middle of the Alaskan wilderness, you shouldn't expect anyone to come to your rescue.

All in all, the Iditarod Invitational is designed for the hardiest of the hardy. The race organizer is Alaska Ultra Sport (www.alaskaultrasport .com), an adventure and guiding company that also offers winter training camps for those who want to test their mettle before venturing onto the trail.

Billiken: Alaska's Good Luck Charm
Nome

It's not fuzzy like a rabbit's foot. You can't hunt for it the way you'd search for a four-leafed clover. The chubby, pointy-headed, grinning Billiken is Alaska's own unique good luck charm.

It all began a long ways from Alaska, when an art teacher from Kansas City, Missouri, patented the cartoonish image that became known as a Billiken in 1908. All sorts of things were manufactured bearing the Billiken's likeness: dolls, coin banks, little statues. Called "the god of things as they ought to be," Billikens were hugely popular for half a year, and then, as is the way with fads, interest faded.

But Alaska's not so worried about what's popular everywhere else. The Buddha-like Billiken made its way north, perhaps when they were used to market the region in the Alaska-Yukon-Pacific Exposition. On

* *

**An ivory Billiken made by a local
Nome craftsman**
PHOTO BY B. B. MACKENZIE

Little Diomede Island, where on some days it actually is possible to
see Russia from your house, a storekeeper introduced the Billiken to a
famed native carver nicknamed Happy Jack.

The figures became popular with tourists, and before long they
became associated with Alaska and were assumed to have originated
here. Native carvers reportedly find them rather uninteresting to make,
but they are relatively quick, easy, and economical because scraps of
ivory can be used. Because the Alaskan Billikens aren't mass produced
as the originals were, some features have been streamlined, with India
ink used to add detail, as is typical on most ivory carved in Alaska.

★ ★

Small variations occurred over the years. Billikens with large ears and folded legs began to appear, and some of the Billiken heads got more pointy. Some are now purported to be female "millikens" with red smiles instead of black, and a few custom X-rated Billikens were carved for servicemen stationed in Northwest Alaska during World War II. The image proliferated in carved trinkets from cuff links to earrings to pipes to salt and pepper shakers.

Various stories arose about how to get the most luck out of a Billiken, with some claiming you had to pretend to have "borrowed" rather than purchased the Billiken, and others going so far as to say that you got the best luck from a stolen Billiken—though that contention rather quickly fell out of favor.

Thanks to Alaska, Billikens never completely fell out of favor, and in recent years, they have been replicated in Russia, Japan, and other unlikely places. Nome is one of the best places to find authentic Alaska Billikens. Look for the little good luck guys at the Arctic Trading Post, 302 Front Street (907-443-2686) or Jim's Ivory Shop, 211 Front Street (907-443-2335).

The Ice Age Lingers
Nome

The saber-toothed tiger, the woolly mammoth, the mastodon, the giant sloth—all disappeared at the end of the Ice Age. Not so for the musk ox, Pleistocene survivor of the Arctic.

Once prevalent throughout the Northern Hemisphere, musk oxen retreated to the farthest north parts of the world at the end of the Ice Age. Today they roam parts of Greenland, Scandinavia, Siberia, and Canada. They had to be reintroduced to Alaska in the 1930s after being wiped out in the late 1800s. Stock from Greenland was first stabilized on Nunivak Island in Southwest Alaska and then distributed to other parts of the state, including nearby Nelson Island, Wrangell Island, the Seward Peninsula, and the Arctic National Wildlife Refuge.

**Musk oxen along the roadside near Nome, on the
Seward Peninsula in Northwest Alaska**
PHOTO BY G. M. FERENCY

Musk oxen are neither musky nor oxen but are most closely related
to sheep and goats. Scientists say they've changed little since the days
of the Ice Age. Both males and females have horns, and they have two
layers of fur that make them impervious to both cold and mosquitoes.
Their soft fur underlayer, called qiviut, is shed in the spring and gathered by native women to be spun into a soft yarn that is four times
warmer than wool.

Animal researchers report that the behavior of musk oxen resembles
that of elephants in some respects. Harem groups form during the
mating season, led by one male that keeps others away. Bulls will

★ ★

charge one another during the rut, their thick skulls protecting them from what would otherwise be deadly impact. To protect their young and vulnerable, musk oxen will huddle in either a line or a circle, with each animal facing the predator, a defense that works well with pack animals like wolves but not with armed hunters.

With stubby legs, musk oxen aren't built for migrating. Instead, they hunker down in cold Arctic winters. A whole standing herd on occasion

Alaska's Fiddling Poet

Alaska has a longstanding musical heritage, from traditional native dancing to Athabascan fiddling to modern artists like Jewel, who grew up in Homer. Among the more unusual musicians our state has produced is fiddling poet Ken Waldman.

Drawing on twenty-five years of Alaska experience, including quite a lot in the Bush, Waldman is an Alaskan troubadour with his fiddle. He's on the road a good part of the year, performing onstage with stories, poems, and fiddle tunes. A former college professor, Waldman clearly has fun with his children's books and old-time string-band music.

Appalachia meets Alaska in Waldman's creative work. He's known for putting on entertaining shows that draw content from his Alaskan adventures and infuse poetry with new energy. After nine CDs and over eight hundred shows in forty-six states, Waldman has written about his experiences, including a 1996 plane crash near Nome, in a memoir called *Are You Famous?*

will become drifted over with snow. During harsh conditions, their metabolic rates and their oxygen consumption will drop them into a state of "standing hibernation."

If you can't get to the Bush to see musk oxen roaming free, you can see them at the University of Alaska's Large Animal Research Station on Yankovich Road in Fairbanks and also at the privately owned Musk Ox Farm at mile 50 of the Glenn Highway in Palmer.

Ken Waldman, Alaska's fiddling poet
PHOTO BY KATE WOOL

Fish Wheels

When most of us think of fishing, we think of rods, reels, and lines. While there's plenty of that type of angling going on in our waters, Alaska is also home to a unique type of fishing: by wheel.

Fish wheel technology was brought to Alaska from the West Coast during the nineteenth century and was quickly adopted by Alaska natives as a means of harvesting salmon. Like a water-powered paddle wheel, a fish wheel consists of paddles and baskets that turn in the current, capturing fish and dumping them into a holding pen.

Fish wheels are still used for the subsistence harvest of salmon on the Yukon and Copper Rivers, mostly at remote sites where the current runs fast. They are also used by biologists to count salmon escapement for the determination of harvest limits.

An example of early fish-wheel technology in Alaska
FRANK AND FRANCES CARPENTER COLLECTION, LIBRARY OF CONGRESS

Tundra Tram
Nunapitchuk

Federal highway funds are typically used for repaving, bridges, and
ramps. But if you're trying to cross the tundra of Southwest Alaska,
none of these typical highways components will help. Think outside
the box, though, and repairing the so-called tundra tram is exactly the
type of improvement that makes sense.

The original tundra tram was a cable and wench system put in place
by fur traders during the 1940s to help them get their boats across a
450-foot swath of soggy permafrost between two lakes. It was used
for decades by villagers traveling from their winter homes to spring
and summer camps along Baird Inlet on the Bering Sea coast. Coastal
Yup'ik people use the tram to travel the opposite direction, toward
the hub city of Bethel to access shopping and medical facilities when
the waters at the mouth of the Kuskokwim River are too choppy for a
more direct approach.

After one of the boat ramps faltered and the rusty rails began sinking, administrators in Nunapitchuk, one of the villages closest to the
tram, sought funding for repairs. If all goes according to plan, the
tundra tram will get a facelift, with an extension on each end, treated
ties to hold the rails in place, and interlocking plastic grids to maintain
the trail. The highway project might be somewhat unconventional, but
local residents are pleased that the shortcut will once again help them
save money on gas, which can run nearly twice as high in the Bush as
it does in urban Alaska.

Galapagos of the North
Pribilof Islands

Once the high points of Beringia, the land mass across which humans
and animals migrated from Asia to the Americas over ten thousand
years ago, these two rocky islands in the middle of the Bering Sea
used to harbor millions of fur seals. The islands are quieter now, well
off the beaten path of most tourists and unknown to most Alaskans as

well. They are Saint Paul and Saint George, which together form the Pribilof Islands.

The Aluutiq people of the Aleutian chain tell of a chief's son who once followed fur seals into the fog to their breeding grounds on the islands. When the Russians arrived in the eighteenth century, eager to locate the place where migrating seals spent their summers, the Aluutiq stayed mum, but eventually the uninhabited islands were rediscovered. The Russians then forced Aluutiq sealers from their homes in the Aleutians to the Pribilofs.

Two centuries of exploitation followed, first by the Russians and then by the Americans through various corporate and government-run enterprises. The Pribilof people were at the mercy of their various employers, who offered food, shelter, and services in exchange for their labor, compensation that was inevitably well below market wages.

Though conducive to wildlife, the location of the islands made virtual slaves of the sealers and their families. Not until they were herded aboard a ship and transported to Funter Bay in Southeast Alaska as part of the Aleut internment program during World War II did the Pribilof people become fully empowered to seek better living and working conditions.

The islands today still seem so remote that they might not be part of Alaska at all. In fact, during the statehood debates in the 1950s, there were some in the federal government who argued that the Pribilofs should be held as a separate federal entity because of a 1911 seal treaty, the first international agreement to protect wildlife, a treaty that Alaska would not be constitutionally authorized to uphold.

With declines in sealing, the population of Saint Paul has since fallen to about four hundred people, and there are only eighty or so residents left on Saint George. Still, the villagers maintain a unique and vibrant lifestyle centered on the sea. Industry has shifted to include fishing for halibut, pollock, and cod, and the city of Saint Paul generates some income by storing crab pots for the Bering Sea fishing fleet that travels north from Dutch Harbor each year. Birders visit the islands in hopes of glimpsing rare species that nest there, traveling over seven

The Russian Orthodox Church in Saint Paul on the
Pribilof Islands is over one hundred years old.
PHOTO BY B. B. MACKENZIE

★ ★

hundred miles from Anchorage in small turbo prop planes and braving weather that can leave them stranded for days if not weeks at a time.

It's a way of life in a place that seems almost timeless on a pair of islands unto themselves. In Saint Paul, a subspecies of fox unique to the Pribilofs scamper through town, and an occasional feral cat slinks between houses. No dogs have been allowed on either island since the sealing first

Mastodon Bones

During the last big northern Ice Age ten thousand years ago, American mastodons roamed what is now Alaska and the Yukon Territory. In the millennia since, Alaska's native people have maintained a subsistence lifestyle by harvesting what they could easily access from the region's waters and land.

But prospectors pouring north at the close of the nineteenth century had other ideas. Determined to uncover the region's wealth in gold and precious minerals hidden beneath the earth's surface, they began digging . . . and digging. In the course of their enterprise, it was not uncommon to unearth mastodon bones buried beneath the topsoil, reminders of the ancient beasts that once roamed these parts.

Such finds inspired fanciful tales, one of which was printed in the venerable *New York Times* in 1887, reporting that a native hunter had followed huge tracks into the mountains to a living mastodon. As it turns out, this wasn't the only time a native Alaskan had some fun at the expense of a gullible newcomer. A few years later, a small stampede began outside of Skagway on rumors of gold spread purposefully by local Indians who sold services and supplies to the disappointed prospectors.

began, out of fear that they would harass the seals. The beaches and rocks are littered with seal bones bleached by the sun. At the top of one hill gleams the dome of the Russian Orthodox Church, over a hundred years old, and below it sits the muddy baseball field that's been around since 1911. On Saint George, planes only land if the crosswinds are less than thirty miles per hour, which precludes many days on the Pribilofs.

Miners show off mastodon bones uncovered during their excavations.
FRANK AND FRANCES CARPENTER COLLECTION, LIBRARY OF CONGRESS

Pioneer Igloos

The Moose and Elks have their lodges, the Eagles their aeries. So why not igloos for the Pioneers of Alaska?

The Pioneers are a fraternal organization that strives to preserve the spirit of Alaska's "trailblazers." Igloo Number One was established in Nome in 1907, followed by Igloos in nearby Candle (now a ghost town) and Saint Michael, the Yukon River gateway to the Klondike. In 1908, the three igloos consolidated as the Grand Igloo of the Pioneers of Alaska.

The Pioneers have charged themselves with preserving Alaska's history, along with commemorating those who pioneered the territory in its early years. Other communities convened similar groups, including the Sons of the Northwest in Sitka, the Alaska Pioneers of Kodiak, and the '87 Pioneers Association of Juneau. But it was the Pioneers of Alaska

Pioneer Igloo Number One in Nome
PHOTO BY B. B. MACKENZIE

that spread statewide. Thirty-five Igloo charters have since been convened, along with nineteen auxiliaries, now called Women's Igloos.

It's safe to say that none of Alaska's pioneers took up residence in genuine igloos, which were typically built as emergency shelters by indigenous people who had settled here thousands of years before the pioneers came on the scene. Nor are the Pioneer Igloos to be confused with the state's six Pioneer Homes, one of which is a landmark in Sitka. Alaska's Pioneer Homes are state-operated assisted living facilities for Alaska's elderly.

Home Sweet Octagon
Quinhagak

There are still people who think that residents of Bush Alaska live in igloos. Not so. Alaska's natives built igloos only for emergency shelter, and before they settled in villages with traditional housing, they lived mostly in sod homes.

But the notion of igloos hasn't completely left the Alaska landscape. A prototype round home, much like a yurt, is being heralded as a new innovation in energy-efficient living for Bush Alaska.

The introduction of schools forced Alaska's native people to give up seasonal camps with sod homes that were efficient and warm. Long and hard-to-heat, suburban-style ranch homes became the norm in the villages, but brutal weather conditions have been hard on them. In the village of Quinhagak in Southwest Alaska, deemed the state's most desperate village for housing, drizzling rains and steady winds have led to rotting entryways, swollen walls, and collapsing floors.

Enter the Cold Climate Research Center with a new design that hearkens back to traditional ways. Like a yurt, the octagonal home is easy to heat because there are no hallways, with rooms radiating from the central living space. The exterior walls are made of steel roofing material, with foam sprayed from inside—protected from wet—to insulate against the cold.

The round homes are a lot cheaper to build than boxy ranch-style homes, too. So look for rural housing to return to its roots, minus the snow and the ice.

Dive-Bombing Birds
Unalaska

You know to be wary of bears in the woods. Of moose with their calves. But the stately bald eagle? If you're in Unalaska, you'd best keep an eye out for these dive-bombing birds.

★ ★

In the heart of the Aleutian Islands, Unalaska is more commonly known as Dutch Harbor, the official name of its big commercial fishing port featured on the popular television show *Deadliest Catch*. But it's not the treacherous seas or icy fishing decks that have residents on the alert these days: It's bald eagles on the attack.

Hot and Clean

In many of Alaska's Bush communities, running water is either a new convenience or still not available at all. The problem stems mostly from the lack of funding and infrastructure, though it's exacerbated in many places by permafrost, permanently frozen soils that make normal underground plumbing impossible.

But it turns out you don't need a whole lot of water to get clean—not if you turn up the heat. So in villages throughout Bush Alaska you'll find steambaths, little shedlike structures next to most homes, with chimneys sticking out of the top. Duck inside, shed your clothes, and prepare to get warm—very warm. The stove, often made from a fifty-five-gallon fuel drum, will get red-hot.

On the tundra where there aren't any trees, the fires are stoked with driftwood gathered each spring after breakup, when the rivers deposit trees uprooted from points farther inland. A bucket or two of water, often hauled from the river, sits by the stove. When the fire gets hot enough, the pouring begins. As steam rolls through the dark, closed quarters, the competition begins to see who can outlast the heat. When at last everyone decides they've had as much as they can stand, it's time to lather with soap—at this point you're wet with sweat—and rinse with whatever water is left in the buckets. It's a whole different kind of clean, from the pores out.

★ ★

According to an article in the *Anchorage Daily News,* Unalaska residents have to watch their backs every spring when eagles are nesting. With wingspans up to eight feet, the resident eagles have star power that would make an Alfred Hitchcock bird jealous. Pedestrians walking near the town's post office and clinic have suffered bloody flesh wounds from eagles on patrol.

Eagles mate for life, and they return to their nests year after year. Bald eagles are plentiful in Alaska and were never listed here as endangered like they were in other states. But federal law still prohibits fighting back against our national symbol. Our advice: When you're in Unalaska, dress for protection, and keep an eye on the skies.

Ugliest Catch

Rockfish aren't the prettiest fish in the sea, nor are they the most desirable catch. Yellow-eyed rockfish, also known locally as red snapper, are good eating, but anglers aren't fond of some of their cousins. When the rockfish are hitting, they strike to the point of annoyance, and because some species face certain death when brought to the surface, regulations don't allow for them to be tossed back.

Despite the fact that it was ugly and not the fish they were seeking, the crew of the *Kodiak Enterprise* was happy to keep the shortraker rockfish they caught incidentally off the Pribilof Islands a few years ago. That's because this monster fish was determined to be approximately one hundred years old.

How do you tell the age of a rockfish? Scientists measure the rings of its ear bone.

★ ★

A Riddle

What are the most western, most northern, most eastern, and most southern states in the United States?

For three out of four, think Alaska. Maybe you guessed we're most northern and western (yes, we're farther west than Hawaii). But eastern?

Here's the deal: the islands at the very end of Alaska's Aleutian chain cross the 180th meridian, also known as the international date line, making them technically as far east as you can get.

Most southern we'll concede to our sister state of Hawaii. We can't do it all.

Ballyhoo Mountain
Unalaska

It's not easy to get to, but the reward is stepping into a time warp unlike any other. It starts with either a long flight or a long ferry ride from Anchorage to Unalaska, the official city of Dutch Harbor, home to the Bering Sea fishing fleets made famous by television's *Deadliest Catch* reality series. Get a permit from the local native corporation, Ounalashka, and from behind the ferry dock, set off on the access road to Ballyhoo Mountain.

After a two- to five-hour climb, you'll be at the mountain's thousand-foot summit, from which you'll look down on the city of Unalaska, the Bering Sea, and Makushin Volcano. Once you've had your fill of the view, start exploring the open-air World War II "museum" that includes gun mounts and bunkers connected by

★ ★

Hairy Man

From northern places throughout the world come tales of Sasquatch, or Bigfoot, a human-like creature that stalks the woods on two feet. In the Himalayas, they're Yeti. In China, they're Alma. Among the Athabascans of Interior Alaska, they're Nant'ina, though through most of Alaska, the creature is known simply as the Hairy Man.

Some report that he's shy, while others find him aggressive. There are even reports of Hairy Man couples or families. Some Alaska natives warn their children that if they stray too far or if they're disobedient, they could be captured by a Hairy Man. While there is no hard evidence that the Hairy Man roams Bush Alaska's tundra and forests, anecdotes of close encounters with the creature are passed from person to person.

According to an article in *Alaska* magazine, a high school student at fish camp in Port Graham came across a Hairy Man that whistled and hid in the trees. In the same article, another villager told of a Hairy Man riling his dogs and breaking a window, cutting itself on the glass. In another tale, a Hairy Man was shot, leaving a trail of blood that resembled transmission fluid.

tunnels (bring a flashlight). You'll likely come across 1940s-vintage military canteens, flatware, and soda bottles.

The US military fortified Unalaska and other coastal areas of Alaska in response to the Japanese attack on Pearl Harbor. They stepped up these efforts in a defensive scramble after the Japanese bombed Dutch

Harbor and Unalaska on June 3, 1942. The weather was bad on that day—summer weather in the Aleutians is often foggy and gray—so little damage was done. Three days later, the Japanese invaded the Aleutian island of Kiska, and the next day, the island of Attu. In the Aleutian campaign, sometimes called the "forgotten battle," there were more American casualties attributed to weather-related conditions than due to Japanese fire.

An Upstream Battle
Yukon River

Salmon that fight their way up the Yukon River may make the longest run of any fish in the world. Some species of chum salmon, also known as dog salmon because of their fierce, toothy faces and their mushy meat that's best fed to dogs, migrate 1,678 miles upriver from the ocean to spawn and die.

Not surprisingly, these Upper Yukon River chums don't reach their spawning grounds till well into the fall. Larger and more silver than their lazier cousins, they make their way north after spending up to five years in saltwater. By the time they arrive, the chums' hooked jaws and noses, ragged black stripes, and lumpy backbones make them look like Frankenstein fish.

Celebrating the dogged chums and their fishy cousins is Alaskan artist Ray Troll (see page 31), whose "fin art" (www.trollart.com) includes "Spawn Till You Die" T-shirts. Troll and his wife run the Soho Coho gallery at 5 Creek Street in Ketchikan. From the Yukon, it's the long way around. But that's never stopped a chum salmon.

Starring Christmas

Christmas comes but once a year . . . unless you live in certain Alaskan communities, where it comes twice. That's because the Russian Orthodox Church relies on the old Julian calendar, dropped by Pope Gregory XIII in 1582 to correct a ten-day discrepancy between the solar and calendar years. According to the Julian calendar, Christmas comes on January 7.

Villages with a Russian Orthodox church typically celebrate their January Christmas with a three-day festival called "Slaviq." In Bush Alaska, the celebration is also called "starring" because it involves a processional through the village led by a spinning star. The star is often homemade, decorated with shiny garland and religious pictures.

The festivities begin with a solemn service at the Russian Orthodox church, with men on one side and women on the other. Most worshippers stand—there's limited seating on benches for the elderly and the infirm. After a sermon and a liturgy and the singing of carols, the worshippers parade with the star, stopping first at the home of the church elders, called stalistas.

The entire procession crowds into each home, where they're greeted with a sermon and, in Yup'ik villages, traditional foods like frozen fish, *akutaq* ("Eskimo ice cream" made with shortening, berries, sugar, and sometimes seal oil, mashed potatoes, or fish; see page 230), moose stew, and dried fish. The children bring plastic shopping bags for candy, hauling off loads that rival the best Halloween stash.

Slaviq lasts for three days—and three nights. It becomes an endurance test of sorts, to see who can follow the spinning star till the end.

Diamond in the Bark

Poke around an Alaska gift shop, and you might find a handcrafted stick, lamp, or cane uniquely marked with dark, recessed diamond shapes carved out by fungus.

While diamond willow isn't found only in Alaska, it's more common here than in other parts of the country. Perhaps that's because we have thirty-three varieties of willow. In fact, in parts of the state that are underlain with permafrost, willow is among only a handful of bushes that will grow. At least five of the state's willow species are susceptible to the fungus that causes the diamonds. River banks are good places to find them.

As the host willow grows away from the fungus, diamond-shaped cankers form. These may grow together in regular patterns. As years pass, the diamonds cut deeper into the wood. Affected sapwood can be recognized by bark that is darker and thicker than it is on the rest of the tree. The bark must be peeled back to expose the red-brown diamonds, which grow stronger in color as they are exposed to light.

A stick of ornamental diamond willow
PHOTO BY B. B. MACKENZIE

index

index

index

index

index

about the author

B. B. Mackenzie is the pseudonym for the author of ten Alaska books for children and adults. An Alaskan for over thirty years, she lived in several villages in southwestern Alaska before moving to Fairbanks and then Anchorage. She blogs at www.49writers.blogspot.com and retreats to a riverside cabin whenever she gets a chance.

The author and her assistant
PHOTO BY G. M. FERENCY